Fundamentals of Landscaping and Site Planning

James B. Root

Long, Brown & Associates
Fairfax, Virginia

The AVI PUBLISHING COMPANY, INC.
Westport, Connecticut

Copyright 1985 by
THE AVI PUBLISHING COMPANY, INC.
250 Post Road East
P.O. Box 831
Westport, Connecticut 06881

Library of Congress Cataloging in Publication Data

Root, James B.
  Fundamentals of landscaping and site planning.

  Bibliography: p.
  Includes index.
  1. Landscape architecture.   2. Landscape gardening.
3. Building sites—Planning.   I. Title.
SB472.R795 1985   635.9   85-7554
ISBN 0-87055-477-8

Printed in the United States of America
A B C D 4321098765

Fundamentals
of Landscaping
and Site Planning

"Man and Nature in Harmony with God . . ."

Contents

Introduction

"Landscaping" may be defined as the art of arranging outdoor space for man's use and enjoyment, thereby enhancing the functional and aesthetic quality of that which the eye beholds. The sculpturing of earth forms and the orientation of architectural structures, coupled with the cultivation of soils and the selection and maintenance of vegetative species, entail many disciplines. The material contained herein emphasizes the core curriculum of landscape architecture, namely, the earth sciences, horticulture, and basic design. The combining of such diversified subject matter under one cover is intended to benefit the beginning student of land planning in preparing for more advanced, in-depth studies, to provide a reference manual for the practitioner, and to afford helpful hints for all persons interested in improving their environment.

Effective communication obviously depends on the ability of the communicator. The educational process lacks clarity when the student simply does not comprehend the meaning of a specific word (printed or spoken); the context of thought thus becomes obscured. An attempt has been made in the writing of *Fundamentals of Landscaping and Site Planning* to define technical terms as they appear, thereby facilitating the continuity of interest and/or concentration.

Part I describes the evolution of the earth's surface, its content, and the primary needs and functions of plant life. Various horticultural practices are discussed, pertaining to the establishment of grasses and ornamental trees and shrubs. The basic chemistry of soils and plants is stressed, to the extent satisfying the inquiry of gardening enthusiasts.

Part II introduces the topic of site planning, explaining the concept of contours and the "methodology" of organizing the landscape. Actual classroom problems and professional case studies graphically demonstrate environmental design techniques, emphasizing development of the home grounds. An understanding of art is essential; the basic principles of composition are applied to the structuring of contrasting garden styles.

I

The Basics of Soil
Formation
and Plant
Development

1

Beginning with the Physical World

Students of environmental design (as well as anyone interested in simply growing plants) should become familiar with the fundamental composition and chemistry of the earth. The elements of nature must be understood and appreciated, for they alone govern the survival of vegetative species, without which man would perish. The landscaping process itself is guided by an awareness of earth features and environmental factors that can be modified and those that inherently establish design constraints. Professional land planners obviously are influenced by the sometimes immovable and irrepressible forces of the physical world. The formidable arrangements of various rock stratifications often determine the twist of a roadway; prevailing winds and solar intensities are key factors affecting the selection of sites and the subsequent orientation of structures. Where to build and what to plant are dependent upon the character of the earth's crust, basic insight regarding soil behavior, and, of course, climatic considerations. It is the author's intent in this chapter to describe briefly the evolution and structure of the earth's outer shell. Though seemingly dull reading at first glance, such knowledge is necessary for the aspiring practitioner. Actually, the study of the earth sciences is most fascinating when one realizes the chemical similarities in the make-up of people, plants, and earth materials.

The Origin of Inorganic Earth Matter

Originally our planet was a molten mass, spinning, rotating, spewing, fuming, and, finally, cooling, thus asserting itself in the universe. In its molten state, the earth was believed to have consisted of a liquid rock-producing material, called "magma," coupled with heavier metallic substances. During the process of cooling, the heavier material settled to the earth's interior, forming what generally is regarded to be an iron–nickel core. The solidification of magma near the earth's exterior produced intrusive (subsurface) igneous rocks, notably granite. Through volcanism, magma and perhaps solid rock forms were thrust to the earth's surface, generating lava flows. Eventually, the cooled lava resulted in the formation of extrusive igneous rocks, the most common being basalt. The parent (igneous) rocks thus formed were metamorphosed, that is, altered physically and chemically by subsurface heat, pressure, and/or steaming fluid, and decomposed through the ages by surface weathering, thereby yielding sediments such as sand, gravel, and clay. Again, through eons of weather cycles and earth upheavals, the conglomeration of sand produced sandstone, and the compaction of clay formed shale. As a parent sedimentary rock, shale may have undergone further metamorphism, thus producing slate. The terms "igneous," "sedimentary," and "metamorphic" refer to various stages of rock evolution.

Igneous rocks, then, are the primary formations consisting of solidified magma. Igneous materials comprise about 85% of the earth's crust. Sedimentary rocks evolve from the eventual compaction of residual particles, or sediments, of previous rock outcroppings that have been eroded. Sedimentary materials are associated with glacial deposits and alluvial soils. Metamorphic rocks are those materials—either igneous, sedimentary, or metamorphic—that have been further modified by folding and faulting.

A cross-section of the earth could be compared to that of a golf ball. The folding, faulting planetary shell is analogous to the tough, resilient outer covering of the ball; the golf ball dimples suggest craters and imaginary bodies of water. The seemingly endless maze of tightly wound elastic strands occupying most of the golf ball interior is comparable to the preponderance of earth's liquid magma. And, the inner sphere, usually rubber, sometimes steel, around which the strands are wrapped somewhat resembles the presumed metallic center of our planet.

Terms to Be Used

A certain amount of technical jargon is essential in order to understand the basic inorganic chemistry of the physical world. There is just no other way to explain the microscopic activity involved in the formation of soils and the ultimate growing of plants (organic chemistry). A dictionary should always be available and referred to whenever the meaning of a particular word or word concept is not clear. The following definitions are of primary significance.

Element: A fundamental substance consisting of homogeneous atoms. There are approximately 100 chemical elements known to exist in the universe, either singly or in combination constituting all matter.

Atom: The smallest unit of an element that can exist alone or in combination, though atoms are believed to consist of still smaller electrically charged particles. Systematically, the negative charges (electrons) move about a nucleus of positive charges (protons) and closely associated neutrons (neutral, or balanced charges) (Fig. 1.1).

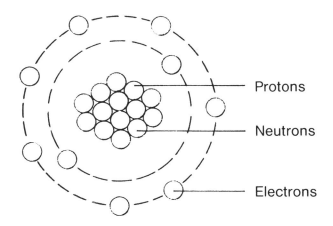

Fig. 1.1. Hypothetical Atom

Valence: The capacity of atoms to unite, one to another. According to modern theory, the degree of valence, or combining power, depends on the number and arrangement of the electrons composing the outermost shell of an atom.

Compound: A distinct substance formed by the union of two or more elements.

Oxide: The combination of oxygen with another element.

Dioxide: An oxide having two atoms of oxygen per molecule, an example being carbon dioxide (CO_2).

Molecule: The smallest quantity of an elemental substance or compound that, when separated from the substance, retains chemical identity with the substance in mass. For example, a molecule of water, consisting of two atoms of hydrogen and one atom of oxygen, retains the same chemical formula as water en masse (H_2O).

Mineral: A naturally occurring inorganic (non-living) substance having a definite chemical composition. Minerals, either as a single element or as compounds, usually are solids, with the exception of liquid water and mercury at normal temperatures. Minerals commonly possess a definite molecular structure, manifested in crystalline form.

Crystal: A substance having a regularly repeating internal arrangement of its atoms, often revealing plane surfaces externally; hence, crystalline.

Rock: A mixture of minerals; consequently, the physical and chemical composition of rocks varies with the characteristics of the constituent minerals.

Silica: (Silicon dioxide) A chemical compound of the elements silicon and oxygen (SiO_2), generally being suspended in water (colloidal solution). Upon continued coagulation and hydration, silica forms a series of substances, quartz being the ultimate anhydrous manifestation.

Alumina: An oxide of aluminum (Al_2O_3), being a major constituent of feldspar, and eventually, clay.

Composition of Basic Rock Materials

The essential chemical elements comprising the earth's upper crust are oxygen (47%), silicon (27%), and aluminum (8%). The atoms of various elements unite to form compounds, or minerals, which in turn form rocks. The vast majority of mineral and rock formations are classified as "silicates," denoting a preponderant mixture of the above, along with admixtures of other elements. Quartz (oxygen and silicon) and feldspar (oxygen, silicon, and aluminum) are the chief mineral components of granite. Granite, mentioned earlier as an igneous rock, decomposes to yield gravel, sand, and eventually silt (residual particles of quartz). White silica sand frequently can be seen lining golf course traps. Clays consist primarily of silica and alumina (residual particles of feldspar). Gravel, sand, silt, and clay represent the basic rock fragments constituting soils.

A mixture of carbon and oxygen produces various "carbonates." Calcium carbonate constitutes the widespread mineral known as calcite, and, with the addition of magnesium (carbonate), dolomite. Calcite and dolomite are the principal components of limestone. Metamorphosed limestone lends itself to the evolution of marble. Interestingly, pure carbon may yield diamonds, the hardest of all minerals; talc, derived from a combination of magnesium and silica, represents the softest. Iron oxides also constitute a significant grouping of earth materials.

Figure 1.2 shows the formation of carbonates and silicates, indicating rocks that perhaps are most commonly observed.

Characteristics of Various Stones Used in Construction

Various stones and rock particles obviously possess unique qualities, and thus become identified with specific functions in the building trades. The strength of granite is a highly desirable structural attribute. Limestone and sandstone, characterized by durability and workability, commonly are employed in the construction industry. The beauty of marble lends itself to ornamental exteriors. Slate serves well as a roofing material. Bluish sandstone (bluestone) and slate are used as flagging or paving materials for walks, sometimes employed as copings for retaining walls. Sand, of course, is an ingredient of mortar, the bonding material for masonry; gravel, as an additive to mortar, becomes a constituent of concrete. Pea gravel may be preferred as a surface material for driveways.

The crushing strength of a rock is the load that it can resist without distortion, and may vary from 15 to 1800 tons per square foot. In building construction, the crushing load is divided by a figure termed the "safety factor," arbitrarily ranging from 2 to 10; the quotient represents the allowable weight (per square foot) of a proposed structure with reference to a particular soil (rock) foundation. That is to say, if the existing rock formation on a given site can support a crushing load of perhaps 60 tons per square foot, then it should safely support a building weighing from 6 to 30 tons per square foot, depending on the safety factor chosen. Generally, noncompressible, sound rock stratifications should support a weight of from 8 to 60 tons per square foot. Tests to determine the actual bearing capacity of a specific site should be conducted for all major construction, in accordance with local building codes and accepted architectural–engineering practices.

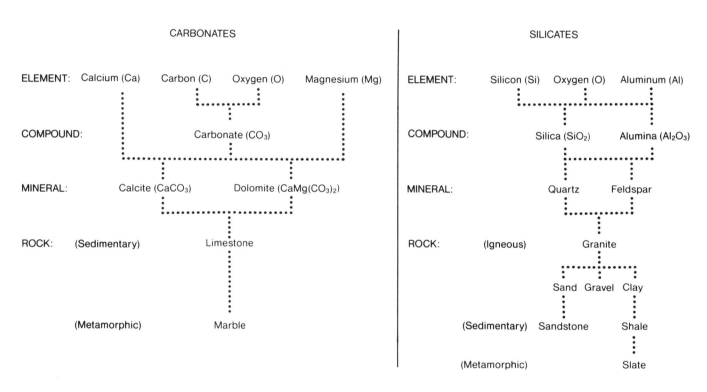

Fig. 1.2.   Rock Formation

Soil Composition and Structure

Soils may be defined as a growing medium for plants, assuming the soil is productive. The five principal components of soils are *minerals* (residual rock particles); *microscopic organisms* (animal and/or plant); *humus* (decaying organic matter); *water;* and *air.* Structurally, soils are classified according to constituent particle size.

Gravel: 2.0 mm or more in diameter (1 mm equals 0.039 in.).

Sand: 0.05–2.0 mm (0.5–20 particles per millimeter, or 13–520 particles per inch).

Silt: 0.002–0.05 mm (20–500 particles per millimeter, or 520–13,000 particles per inch).

Clay: 0.002 mm or less (500 or more particles per millimeter, or 13,000 or more particles per inch).

Humus comprises decomposed particles of organic matter in various stages of carbonization (conversion to a residue). Peat refers to decomposed matter in which the parent material can be identified; muck consists of unrecognizable particles of plant remains.

Soil Horizons

In profile, soils may exhibit clearly discernible zones of weathering, known as soil horizons (Fig. 1.3):

The *A Horizon* (topsoil) extends to a depth of perhaps 10–20 in. Intense weathering occurs, with a high probability of leaching (removal of water-soluble nutrients and clay particles as soil moisture filters downward).

The *B Horizon* is a zone of moderate weathering, extending another 12–20 in. Accumulations of leached material from the A Horizon may appear.

The *C Horizon* (subsoil) undergoes very little weathering, and measures perhaps 18–24 in. in thickness.

The *D Horizon* consists of unaltered bed rock masses (granite, limestone, sandstone, shale, etc.).

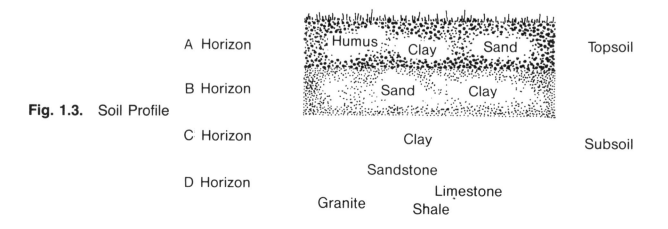

Fig. 1.3. Soil Profile

The depths of soil horizons vary considerably throughout the world. It must be remembered that the invaluable topsoil necessary for human survival often is precariously thin, perhaps even nonexistent. From the standpoint of soil productivity, the A Horizon should be friable and fertile, exhibiting a dark brown appearance (containing humus). The B Horizon essentially is composed of yellowish clay particles, varying somewhat according to climate, topography, geological age, and parent rock material. Red-yellow rust-like colorations in soils are indicative of iron oxides and hydroxides (iron—hydrogen—oxygen compounds).

The intermittency of alternating, contrasting weather cycles through the ages has tempered our planet to the shape in which it manifests itself today. Life forms and inorganic masses, the intricate system of substance, lies before us, many of its mysteries yet unsolved, its rhythmic patterns of perpetual transformation eluding the comprehension of man. The ever-changing process of chemical interactions is extremely complex; it suffices for environmental planners, however, to limit inquiries to those of fundamental considerations. The foregoing introductory statements merely suggest specialized areas of concentration for further studies regarding the earth sciences.

2

The Miracle of
Plant Life

Essential Chemical Elements

The chemical elements known to exist in the universe are the atomic constituents, in various combinations, or formulas, of any substance, whether gaseous, liquid, solid, inorganic, or organic. For example, the carbon found in diamonds, coal, and graphite (inorganic masses) is a constituent of *all* living compounds as well. Fifteen basic chemical elements are considered essential for plant life, with perhaps chlorine being the sixteenth. Carbon, oxygen, hydrogen, nitrogen, phosphorus, potassium, calcium, magnesium, and sulfur comprise the macronutrients—elements required in abundance. The elements required in lesser amounts (micronutrients) are iron, manganese, zinc, copper, boron, and molybdenum.

Carbon

The primary structural substance of organic forms, carbon accounts for approximately 50% of the dry weight of plants. It is available from carbon dioxide in the atmosphere, which results from the burning (oxidation) and release of energy in both plants and animals. The total process is referred to as "respiration." The transformation or exchange of elements, due to ionic attraction, is the phenomenon of existence; carbon and oxygen, for instance, unite, separate, and reunite in a continuous cycle of creation and destruction.

Oxygen

A major constituent of the rock-forming carbonate–silicate compounds, oxygen comprises about 40% of the dry weight of plants. It is obtainable from both air and water, water itself accounting for 60–90% of the *total* weight of plants.

Hydrogen

Its principal source being water, hydrogen comprises about 6% of plant compounds (dry weight). (Pure water by weight contains 88% oxygen, 12% hydrogen.) Carbon, oxygen, and hydrogen are the primary components of nonliving plant tissue–cell walls, intracellular starch grains, etc.—in addition to other structural constituencies. Nitrogen, phosphorus, potassium, calcium, magnesium, and sulfur essentially exist as colloidal particles, contributing to the function and growth of plant life.

Nitrogen

A constituent of the chlorophyll molecule, nitrogen is important in vegetative development. Nitrogen atoms are derived both from atmospheric gases and decomposed organic matter in the soil. The availability of soluble nitrogen to the roots of living plants involves a series of transformations.

Lightning unites nitrogen and oxygen; the resultant nitrogen oxides permeate the soil during a rainfall. Simple plant forms, known as "nitrogen fixers" (various algae, fungi, and bacteria), ingest the oxides. The total process is referred to as "nitrogen fixation."

Decaying organic matter in the soil contains nitrogenous compounds (protein nitrogen), which cannot be absorbed by plants. Certain fungi and bacteria (ammonifiers) feed on the protein nitrogen, converting it to ammonia (hydrogen and nitrogen). This process is called "ammonification." Other bacteria (nitrifiers) convert ammonia nitrogen first to nitrite nitrogen, then to nitrate nitrogen, the form of nitrogen most readily available to root systems. The latter process is called "nitrification."

Box-like microscopic plant cells, approximately the size of clay particles, are the basis for all life. Essentially, inorganic atoms are assembled from the atmosphere and/or soil solution, converted to living matter within the cell, and perhaps again relegated to nonliving cell structures. Some elements simply serve as catalysts, or enzymes, for the creation of organic compounds, while others become basic constituents of the life substances.

In combination with carbon, oxygen, and hydrogen, nitrogen is a major constituent of proteins, a primary component of the living cell substance called "protoplasm." An outer covering, the cell wall, protects the protoplasmic content (water, 85–90%; proteins, 5–10%; and other organic–inorganic materials), within which the life-sustaining processes of metabolism occur.

The significant parts of a cell are illustrated in Fig. 2.1.

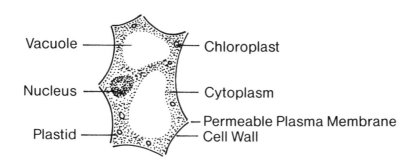

Fig. 2.1. Simplified plant cell

The following terms are useful in understanding the physiological processes within plants, especially the leaves.

Protoplasm: The living substance of plants and animals.

Protoplast: The plant cell, exclusive of the nonliving cell wall.

Cytoplasm: The protoplasm within the cell, exclusive of the nucleus, plastids, and other protoplasmic structures of somewhat definite form; essentially, the protoplasmic fluid in which plastids and the nucleus are suspended.

Nucleus: A substance appearing in all cells as a grayish mass, serving to coordinate various functions.

Plastids: Specialized colloidal protoplasmic bodies within the cytoplasm, some being green (chloroplasts), some red-yellow (chromoplasts), and some colorless (leucoplasts).

Chloroplast: A plastid containing chlorophyll, within which photosynthesis takes place.

Chlorophyll: The green, light-absorbing substance of plants, associated with carotene (a red-yellow substance) and xanthophyll (a brown-yellow substance), also found in chloroplasts.

Vacuoles: Storage sacs or reservoirs containing a watery solution of sugars and other materials.

Photosynthesis: The combining of carbon dioxide and water (in the presence of light; hence, the prefix, photo-) to form basic foodstuffs.

The permeable cell wall admits water when the outside concentration exceeds that within the cell by a process referred to as "osmosis." Soluble minerals similarly diffuse into root hairs. The retention of water within cells generates "turgor pressure;" hence, leaf rigidity. The protoplasmic fluid (cytoplasm) normally is in motion, and may be transmitted from one cell to another through the outer "plasma membrane." Vacuoles likewise are protected by the "vacuolar membrane," which selectively permits the exchange of matter with the surrounding cytoplasm.

Phosphorus

A constituent of protoplasm (sometimes occurring in proteins), phosphorus contributes directly to root development and the production of flowers, seed, and fruit. Phosphorus appears naturally in combination with calcium and oxygen as phosphate rock. Chemically treated with sulfuric acid, phosphate rock produces superphosphate, the principal commercial source of phosphorus.

Potassium

Potassium promotes root development, resistance to cold weather, and the general health and vigor of plants. The principal sources are the soluble chemical compounds known as potassium chloride (KCl), a mixture of potassium and chlorine occurring as the mineral sylvite, and potassium sulfate (K_2SO_4), a mixture of potassium, sulfur, and oxygen.

Calcium

In the form of a substance known as calcium pectate, calcium strengthens cell walls. The minerals *calcite* (calcium, carbon, and oxygen) and *dolomite* (calcite plus magnesium carbonate) are primary natural sources. The calcium and sulfate content of soils may be increased without raising the pH level (see Chapter 3) by incorporating gypsum.

Magnesium

This constituent of chlorophyll, as part of the magnesium–pectate molecule, assists in the formation of cell walls. Native magnesium occurs in dolomitic limestone.

Sulfur

This constituent of certain proteins assists in the formation of chlorophyll. To become available as a plant nutrient, sulfur must be oxidized, that is, combined with oxygen. Protein sulfur in decaying plants is converted to the usable sulfate form (SO_4) by soil organisms, a process called "sulfofication", similar to nitrification. Atmospheric sulfur is washed into the soil by rainfall. Superphosphate contains sulfur, resulting from the sulfuric acid treatment, and thus becomes a commercial source. Ammonium sulfate is a common fertilizing ingredient.

It is generally presumed that organisms cannot survive without carbon, oxygen, hydrogen, and nitrogen, the primary protoplasmic ingredients. The planetary presence of methane, a hydrocarbon referred to as "marsh gas", ammonia, hydrogen, and/or water, then, lends itself to speculation about biological evolution. Theoretically, solar radiation synthesized amino acids (see Chapter 3) from these elements, resulting in a kind of "thick soup," from whence life emerged.

Simple Plant Forms

The simplest food-producing forms of plant life are known as "algae." They are mostly single-celled organisms containing chlorophyll but lacking roots, stems, and leaves. Examples range from the green film often found on outdoor fixtures to seaweed. "Fungi" (molds, mushrooms, etc.) are likewise simple structures, characteristically lacking chlorophyll and so must derive energy from other forms of matter. Parasitic fungi feed on living organisms, while saprophytes obtain food from organic remains. Bacteria are a type of unicellular organisms that may derive energy from the oxidation (chemosynthesis) of inorganic compounds. Algae may coexist with and sustain certain fungi, forming lichens, frequently appearing on rocks and tree trunks. All these simple plants propagate either through cell division, called "fission," or the formation of spores, which are minute reproductive protoplasmic bodies.

"Mosses" presumably evolved from algae, possessing structures resembling stems and leaves. Hair-like rhizoids extend from the base of the plants, serving to anchor the moss clusters and absorb water and mineral nutrients. "Ferns" exhibit definite roots, stems, and leaves, as well as containing vascular or conducting systems for the transport of water, minerals, and manufactured food. Mosses and ferns reproduce by spores.

Higher Plant Forms

Higher forms of plant life (seed plants) are classified as "gymnosperms" (having exposed seeds attached to the female cones of various perennial evergreen trees and shrubs) and "angiosperms" (possessing enclosed seeds within the fleshy or pod-like fruit of flowering annuals, biennials, and perennials). The plant embryo within the seed of angiosperms may consist of either one or two nutrient storehouses, called "cotyledons." Grass seed contains one cotyledon, and therefore (the plant) is further classified as a monocotyledon, or simply, monocot. Dicotyledons, or dicots, contain two cotyledons (Fig. 2.2), representative of most ornamental plant material.

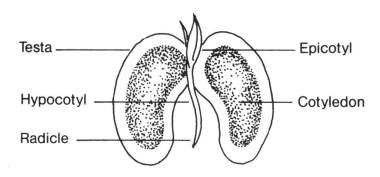

Fig. 2.2. Dicot seed (open view)

Dicot Seed Structure

An elongated, embryonic structure lies between the cotyledons of a dicot seed, the lower portion being the "hypocotyl" and the upper portion being the "epicotyl." The tip of the hypocotyl, called the "radicle," develops into the primary root. The epicotyl (plumule), often bearing miniature leaves within the seed coating (testa), develops into the stem and leaves of the growing plant, and later, flowers and fruit. The cotyledons remain attached to the base of the epicotyl (sometimes emerging above ground) until the food reserves are depleted and the seedling begins to utilize soil nutrients.

"Germination" may be defined as the resumption of active life from a dormant state. The germination period generally refers to the time required for an above-ground response after the planting of seeds. The appearance of surface vegetation depends on favorable levels of soil oxygen and water, coupled with warming temperatures. Fertilization supplements the soil nutrients and helps sustain the early growth process.

Tree Structure

The stem or trunk of a tree (Fig. 2.3) contains a dark central core known as "heartwood," a nonliving sapless material yielding structural support. Surrounding the heartwood lies the light-colored sapwood, a group of cells known as the "xylem," serving to conduct water and nutrients to the upper reaches of the tree. The sapwood is ringed by the "cambium," a thin band of living tissue responsible for growth.

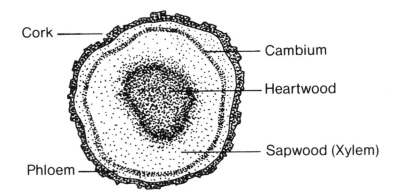

Fig. 2.3. Stem (trunk) section

The stem is protected by a two-layered substance commonly referred to as "bark," the exposed portion (cork) consisting of nonliving, water-impervious cells. The inner layer contains the "phloem," a group of cells serving to transport manufactured sugar in leaves downward to the roots and stem. The cambium lies between the phloem and the inner sapwood (xylem), contributing to the cell formation of both, accompanied by the stretching and cracking of existing bark (as the tree expands outward).

Leaves consist of the flattened blade attached to a stalk or petiole (Fig. 2.4). The surfaces on either side of the blade are called the "epidermis," a transparent covering between which lie the chloroplast-containing mesophyll cells. Porous

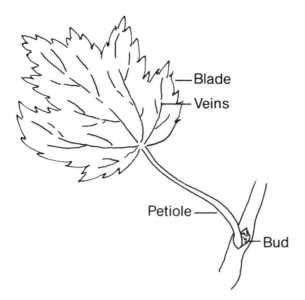

Fig. 2.4. Leaf structure

openings within the epidermis are called "stomata." The stomata, generally located on the underside of the blade, are surrounded by "guard cells," which control the size of the leaf perforations.

Floral Parts

The floral parts of a flower (Fig. 2.5) rest upon the stem tip, called the "receptacle." Encircling the receptacle are the sepals, collectively referred to as the "calyx." The petals, collectively called the "corolla," are positioned inside the sepals. The colorful petals usually are scented with nectar, produced in nectaries at the base of the petals. Together, sepals and petals constitute the "perianth." The "pistil" (sometimes more than one) occupies the center of the flower cluster. It consists of the stigma (uppermost part), the elongated central style, and the basal ovary. "Stamens" encircle the pistil(s), and consist of the filament, or stalk, and the anther.

Pollen is produced in the anther; hence, the stamens are referred to as the male organs. Reproduction occurs in the fertilized ovary of the female pistil.

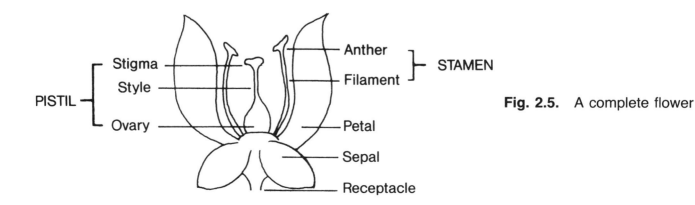

Fig. 2.5. A complete flower

The *"complete"* flower contains all floral parts (sepals, petals, stamens, and a pistil). *"Incomplete"* flowers lack one or more of the floral parts. A *"perfect"* flower contains stamens and at least one pistil. *"Imperfect"* flowers contain either the pistil (pistillate flowers) or stamens (staminate flowers), but not both. Furthermore, plants bearing both pistillate and staminate flowers are known as "monoecious" plants. "Dioecious" plants contain only pistillate or staminate flowers, respectively, on a single specimen. Floral descriptions, then, can become somewhat complex; a flower may be incomplete, yet perfect.

This terminology is of practical concern to those involved in fruit production and/or plant propagation. Also, landscape gardeners must understand the nature of dioecious plant material and the need to juxtapose, or group, male and female specimens of the same species in order to increase the production of berries. Interestingly, a twig containing staminate flowers may be grafted to a dioecious plant bearing pistillate flowers, thereby accommodating self-pollination.

An in-depth study of plant sexuality is, of course, beyond the scope of this book. Simply stated, "sexual" reproduction involves the union of sex cells, called "gametes." Most forms of vegetation, including certain algae and bacteria, are capable of sexual reproduction. "Asexual" reproduction does not involve the fusion of gametes, but rather, multiplication by cell division, the development of specialized spores, and such artificial means as budding, grafting, layering, cutting, and root separation.

The vast majority of deciduous trees and flowering shrubs consists of dicots. Typical monocots are lilies, irises, orchids, palms, and a variety of grasses, sedges, and rushes. The identity of monocots and dicots may be evidenced by outward signs; the leaf veins of the former are paralleled, and the floral parts are arranged in multiples of three, while the leaf veins of dicots are net-like in appearance, and the respective floral parts number in multiples of four or five.

Photosynthesis

The process of photosynthesis is a highly complex function of plant life. Water and various solutes, notably magnesium and sulfur, are transported by the xylem from the root system to the chloroplasts through leaf veins. Carbon dioxide enters the leaf through the stomata. Within the chloroplasts, which are food-manufacturing centers, carbon dioxide combines with water to form *glucose.* The sugary substance then is transported to other parts of the plant through the phloem. Mankind not only depends on the carbohydrates thus synthesized, but likewise owes its existence to the oxygen released by the leaf as a by-product.

The three groups of food manufactured by plants are carbohydrates, fats, and proteins. "Carbohydrates" contain carbon, hydrogen, and oxygen. Water-soluble forms are known as sugars (like energy-producing glucose), while water-insoluble carbohydrates at normal temperatures comprise starch and *cellulose,* a major component of cell walls.

"Fats" and oils are derived from carbohydrates, being somewhat deficient in oxygen. Essentially, fats are solid and oils are liquid, both serving as stored energy for living cells.

"Proteins" consist of carbon, hydrogen, oxygen, and nitrogen, with some iron, phosphorus, and/or sulfur. The combining of glucose and nitrogen to form proteins may occur at any time, as opposed to the daylight process of photosynthesis.

Photosynthesis, cell division, and reproduction are the basic biological processes responsible for the seasonal function and development of plants. Cell division, occurring primarily in the meristematic or growth tissue of the root system, the cambium, the buds, and the stem tip, involves the separation of the cell nucleus and the concurrent build-up of distinct cell walls for each half; thus, two cells. (It must be noted that this and other discussions of plant physiology are oversimplified; the intention merely is to acquaint the reader with fundamental concepts.)

Plant Life Cycle

Buds are found on branches and twigs at the base or node of existing leaf petioles and/or fruit stems, having emerged after the flowering period of the current year's growth. Those at the tip of a branch are known as "terminal" buds; those flanking the branches, "axillary" buds. Development continues within the protective sheath throughout the summer months. During late fall, buds enter a period of dormancy. With the warmth of spring, the bud scales fold back, revealing infant leaves and/or flowers.

The scent of nectar in the newly formed blossoms attracts bees and other insects, giving rise to cross-pollination. Midsummer functions involve the development of fruit and the continual synthesis of basic foods within the leaf.

During late summer and early fall fruits are harvested or left on the plant. At this time the seeds within the angiospermic fruit and the new buds enter their rest period, anticipating the cool days of winter. The sap flow to leaves is greatly reduced (triggered by a combination of shorter daylight hours and lower temperatures), causing the cork-like tissue at the base of petioles to dry out. Subsequently, the chlorophyll content of chloroplasts is diminished, exposing the more drought-resistant pigments, carotene and xanthophyll. Thus, the yellow autumnal colorations in leaves signal the end of another growth cycle.

To summarize the basic biochemical, biophysical processes within plants, one might compare photosynthesis with respiration, and water absorption with transpiration. Photosynthesis creates a food supply, vital to plant metabolism. The use of food and the subsequent release of energy (respiration), represents the reverse process of photosynthesis. Growing plants demand an abundance of food reserves; therefore, photosynthesis must exceed the rate of respiration.

Likewise, water is absorbed by the root system, and released through the stomata (transpiration). Water absorption must at least equal transpiration, else the leaves lose turgor, the guard cells shrink, closing the stomata, and photosynthesis is curtailed by the reduced intake of carbon dioxide. Furthermore, vapor loss cools the plant during hot summer days. With limited water absorption and a subsequent reduction in transpiration, plants become over-heated, and may suffer permanent damage. Healthy plant specimens, then, require favorable soil structures, the proper solar exposure, available nutrients, and a continuous supply of moisture.

The study of botany enriches one's appreciation of the natural environment. An awareness of organic chemistry and plant physiology is essential to those engaged in the production of nursery stock. Certainly, the maintenance of landscapes requires an understanding of plant culture. The miracle of civilization itself could not endure without the food and shelter provided by vegetative species.

3

Soil Conditioning and
Maintenance

Soil Structures Compared

The physical structure of soils determines their capacity to contain air, water, and basic nutrients required for plant life. The porosity of sand permits maximum air penetration to root zones, but at the same time allows excessive drainage, conducive to the rapid decomposition of organic matter. The settlement of soil solutions to lower depths creates a loss of mineral and organic nutrients from the topsoil. This is called "leaching." Clay, on the other hand, retains moisture to the point of becoming water-logged, thus excluding air. In that moisture is held on the surface of soil particles, it becomes evident that clay is more retentive of water than sand, there being more particles of clay, with greater *total* surface area, in a given volume of soil. The eventual drying of clay forms a crust, thus impeding both air and water penetration. The benefit of clay lies in its ability to retain nutrients through the process of ionic (electrical) attraction. Clay particles are negatively charged, and thus "hold" the positively charged atoms vital to the chemistry within plants. Humus contains vegetable remains on which certain soil bacteria feed, making available nitrate nitrogen and other soluble forms of nutrition. Organic matter also retains ions by attraction, thus minimizing leaching.

An ideal garden soil is referred to as "loam;" it contains perhaps 35% sand, 35% silt, 20% clay, and 10% humus. Predominately clay soils can be improved by adding sand. The porosity of sandy soils is counteracted by incorporating sphagnum (bog) peat, a form of humus highly retentive of moisture.

Nutrient Supply

Nature supplies most ordinary soils with the essential plant nutrients. Carbon, oxygen, and hydrogen abound in the atmosphere and/or soil water. Calcium and magnesium are available from soil minerals, and may be supplied with applications of lime. Rainfall usually furnishes adequate quantities of sulfur. Nitrogen, phosphorus, and potassium are likely to be in short supply for vigorous growth, and therefore must be supplemented by the addition of a "complete" fertilizer. The trace elements (micronutrients) very seldom require special attention. Soil testing is essential in determining the chemical composition and physical structure of earth materials. Agricultural extension laboratories at leading universities can be called on to conduct a soil analysis.

Acidity versus Alkalinity

The chemical reaction of soil solutions reflects either an acidic (sour) or alkaline (sweet) quality, depending on the hydrogen (H) concentration. To appreciate the significance of hydrogen is to first understand atomic activity within soil solutions.

The atom contains a magnetic field, an orbital system of electrically charged particles. The central nucleus, serving as the power source, is composed of protons (positive charges) and neutrons (neutral, or balanced charges). Atomic number refers to the total number of protons within the nucleus; atomic weight refers to the number of protons plus the number of neutrons within the nucleus. Concentric orbits of electrons (negative charges) around the nucleus form successive layers, or shells, of electrical motion. When the total number of orbiting electrons equals the number of nuclear protons, the atom is said to be neutral. The outermost shell (valence shell) differs from the interior orbits in that it attracts and dispels (valence) electrons according to the magnetic "pull" of the nucleus. Not only are electrons from various atoms thus exchanged, but the atoms themselves are attracted one to another to form compounds.

When the number of electrons exceeds that of the nuclear protons, a negative charge results. Contrarily, when the atom loses electrons, and the number of protons exceeds the electrons, the atom is positively charged.

The majority of elements are referred to as metals (usually ending in -um or -ium; hence, alumin*um* and calc*ium*), one characteristic being the ability to easily lose electrons; therefore, metals essentially are positively charged. Nonmetals such as oxygen are negatively charged. In a soil solution, the atoms of various elements are subjected to a continuous cycle of exchange.

A molecule of water (H_2O) contains two hydrogen atoms and one oxygen atom. Within the general mass of water, the atoms of some water molecules may dissociate in the form: H^+, O^-, H^+. The negative oxygen atom may again attract, or be attracted by, one of the positive hydrogen atoms, thus forming the hydroxyl compound, OH^-. The remaining hydrogen atom thus becomes a "free" ionic charge in the aqueous solution. The term "ion" denotes an electrically charged atom; hence, atoms and ions may become synonymous references.

Soils are considered acidic because of the dominance of hydrogen ions over hydroxyl ions, measured by a logarithmic scale, known as the "pH" scale, ranging

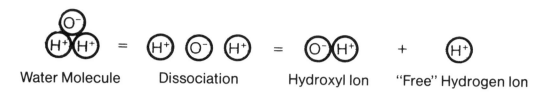

Fig. 3.1. Water ionization

from 0.0–14.0. Below 7.0, the hydrogen ions prevail and the solution is acidic; over 7.0, the hydroxyl ions prevail and the solution is alkaline. A soil solution with a pH of 5 is ten times more acidic than one measuring 6; pH 4.0 reflects acidity one hundred times that of pH 6.0.

Acids are compounds containing (or holding by attraction) the positive hydrogen ion, exchangeable for other positive elements. (Acids containing oxygen end in -ic; when in the process of incorporating increasing amounts of oxygen, -ous.) Examples of strong acid compounds are nitric (HNO_3), being composed of hydrogen, nitrogen, and oxygen; and sulfuric (H_2SO_4), containing hydrogen, sulfur, and oxygen.

Bases are compounds capable of receiving the hydrogen ion as a replacement for another positive charge. They also have the ability to release the hydroxyl ion (OH^-) when dissociated in solution. Examples of bases are various hydroxides (combinations of hydrogen and oxygen, the hydroxyl ion) plus metals such as calcium, iron, and/or potassium.

The water molecule can receive an additional hydrogen ion, thus serving as a base, or it can give up a hydrogen ion, acting as an acid. Pure water, then, is chemically neutral.

Salts are compounds resulting from acids yielding part or all of the hydrogen ions to bases, thus neutralizing the character of both (acids and bases). (Salts resulting from -ous acids end in -ite; those form -ic acids, -ate.) Plant roots absorb nutrients mainly in the form of mineral salts, examples being nitr*ate* nitrogen, superphosph*ate,* and potassium sulf*ate.*

Certain elements may become constituents of acids when subjected to moisture. For instance, atmospheric nitrogen combines with hydrogen and oxygen (catalyzed by lightning) to form free nitric acid (HNO_3). Also, protein nitrogen is converted to nitric acid when exposed to hydrogen and oxygen ions within the soil. Carbon dioxide likewise reacts with aqueous solutions to form carbonic acid (H_2CO_3). Moist sulfur oxidizes to yield sulfuric acid.

Parenthetically, it should be noted that *amino acids* are the structural components of proteins, consisting of carbon, oxygen, hydrogen, nitrogen, and perhaps sulfur. Amino acid molecules, synthesized by plants from certain organic acids and ammonia, characteristically bond together in a chain-like fashion. The resultant proteins contribute to the formation of protoplasm and/or food reserves.

Radicals are groups of atoms that replace a single atom; they form compounds that become fundamental constituents of various substances, remaining unchanged during a series of chemical reactions. The OH ion in water constitutes a radical. Ammonia (NH_3) yields the amino group (radical), NH_2. An amino acid, by definition, is an organic acid in which a portion of the non-acid hydrogen has been replaced by the amino group. Amino acids always contain the NH_2 radical in addition to the carboxyl group (COOH) common to most organic acids, plus other elements. The simplest amino acid, glycine, also contains the hydrocarbon CH_2 and is written NH_2CH_2COOH.

Strong acids release high concentrations of hydrogen ions when dissolved in water. The ionization, or breakdown, of weak acids yields low concentrations of hydrogen. Similarly, bases release hydroxyl ions when dissociated in solution. The neutralization of acids and bases involves the chemical interaction of their respective ions; the free hydrogen and hydroxyl ions merge to form additional water molecules, while the remaining ions unite to produce salts. To illustrate, carbonic acid dissociates readily to produce carbon dioxide (carbonate) and water (H_2O). Nitric acid decomposes into water, nitrogen dioxide (nitrate), and oxygen.

Whether soils are essentially acidic or basic (alkaline) depends on the parent rock material, organic content, and, of course, the presence of moisture. The primary rock constituents, oxygen, silicon, and aluminum, are acidic in character. Sulfuric acid registers less than 2.0 on the pH scale. Clay and sand are composed of acidic particles. Carbonized organic matter lends itself to acidity. On the other hand, iron (5% of the earth's surface layer) combines with hydroxyl ions to form basic compounds. Iron, however, often forms insoluble hydroxide compounds, and should be considered weakly alkaline. Calcium, magnesium, potassium, and sodium hydroxides represent strong bases.

Soil Hydrolysis

Water accelerates the chemical breakdown (hydrolysis) of soil substances. Soil solutions, then, consist of soluble ions from decaying organisms and various minerals, plus the hydrogen and oxygen ions that may have dissociated from the water molecules. The positive and negative ionic charges create a magnetic field in which acidic or basic compounds are formed. Single atoms and radicals are consolidated and again ionized in an ever-changing chemical process. Generally, bases are more susceptible to leaching; therefore, most soil solutions appear to be slightly acidic.

Chemically active sodium is an alkali metal seldom isolated, combining with chlorine to produce common salt (sodium chloride), and with various carbonates, silicates, and sulfates to form constituents of mineral waters and/or rock deposits. Soluble salts accumulate in regions of low precipitation where leaching is minimal. High concentrations of salt limit the intake of water by plant roots. Desert sand, salt flats, limestone, and limited rainfall are associated with alkaline soils, which can be neutralized (pH lowered) by adding aluminum sulfate.

Chemical Translocation

The negative charge of clay particles is responsible for the retention of hydrogen ions in an acidic soil, as well as retaining positive charges of other elements, such as calcium, magnesium, and sodium, in an alkaline soil. The positive ions are held rather loosely at points on the clay particles known as "exchange spots," and readily replace one another.

Plant roots emit carbon dioxide during the respiratory process, thereby producing carbonic acid in soil solutions. The hydrogen ions contained within the acid solution may dissociate and replace other positive ions (cations) held by soil particles. Any nutrients thus released then become available to enter root cells by diffusion.

Nitrates, sulfates, and phosphates are negatively charged compounds containing relatively large amounts of oxygen. The root system therefore may discharge negative hydroxyl ions (anions), to be exchanged in the soil solution for these salts. Essentially, the permeable membrane of the cell wall selectively admits individual atoms when the concentration of a particular nutrient in the soil solution exceeds that within the cell itself. Water molecules likewise are translocated from areas of higher concentration to areas of lower concentration by osmosis. *The diffusion of water and mineral nutrients into root cells are mutually independent functions.*

Soil Fertility and pH Levels

The capacity of soils to accommodate the ionic exchange of minerals, coupled with an adequate supply of available nutrients, determines fertility. In general, slightly acid soils stimulate chemical reactions, and serve to influence the activities of nitrogen-fixing soil bacteria. However, various plants prefer differing pH levels. Horticultural practices involve (1) adapting plants to existing soils, or (2) conditioning the soil to accommodate the desired plant. The latter approach necessitates continued adherence to liming and fertilization schedules.

The pH level of acidity can be raised (neutralized) by the addition of lime. The calcium and sometimes magnesium ions contained in lime are of nutritional value, while serving to replace the hydrogen ions attached to clay particles. It should become apparent that the exchange of positive ions from hydrogen to calcium and other metals to hydrogen again creates pH instability in soils.

Calcareous Minerals

Calcium, carbon, and oxygen are the elemental constituents of the mineral *calcite* ($CaCO_3$). The combination of calcium carbonate (54%) and magnesium carbonate (45%) constitutes the mineral *dolomite*, $CaMg(CO_3)_2$. Limestone consists of calcite, with varying increments of dolomite; dolomitic limestone by definition contains at least 9.5% elemental magnesium. Lime, therefore, may be derived from calcite, dolomite, and/or the limestone rock.

Ordinary ground agricultural limestone normally contains approximately 50% carbonates, 50% oxides; the oxide equivalents (minus carbon) are more basic in character, representing highly active liming agents. Calcite, for example, consists of 56% calcium oxide (CaO) and 44% calcium carbonate (CO_2). Dolomite contains about 30% calcium oxide, 22% magnesium oxide, and 48% calcium–magnesium carbonates. (The magnesium content, in addition to replacing the hydrogen ions on clay particles, assists young seedlings in the formation of chlorophyll. Dolomitic lime should be specified for lawns.)

Liming materials react most effectively when finely ground, thus exposing more particles having greater total surface area. Magnesium especially is slow-reacting as a liming agent, and therefore benefits from pulverization. Specifications should require that 95% of any liming substance pass through a 20-mesh sieve (0.84 mm opening), and 50% through a 100-mesh sieve (0.15 mm opening). Mesh denotes the number of openings per linear inch.

The Manufacture of Lime

When ordinary limestone is subjected to heat (calcined), the union of carbon and oxygen forms carbon dioxide, a gaseous by-product that reduces the carbon content. The remaining calcium oxide is referred to as "quicklime." The addition of water (slaking) to quicklime generates intense heat, the chemical interaction thus producing calcium hydroxide (hydrated lime). The commercial form of hydrated lime is a dry, powdery mass containing approximately 70% calcium oxide. Dolomitic limestone is somewhat difficult to slake, requiring prolonged higher temperatures.

Quicklime and hydrated lime are the more costly forms of liming materials, compared to ordinary ground limestone, but their capacity to neutralize soil acidity likewise is greater. For instance, about 30% less quicklime than the ordinary form is required in a given situation. However, freshly burned limestone, containing as much as 90% calcium oxide, is extremely lumpy, and therefore in part unusable. The powdery form of hydrated lime is preferred, though greater quantities are required as compared to quicklime. Essentially, 65–70 lb of quicklime and about 80 lb of hydrated lime, respectively, are comparable to 100 lb of ordinary ground limestone for effectiveness.

Ground limestone is longer lasting than the hydrated form, and is used generally in agriculture. Hydrated lime is relatively fast-acting for a shorter duration, and may be preferred when establishing lawns on highly acid soils. Follow-up applications should consist of ordinary ground limestone. The caustic (burning) characteristic of hydrated lime is attributable to its high oxygen content; thus, hydrated lime should be applied to soils approximately two weeks prior to seeding. Within that period, the lime should have neutralized the soil and reverted to the nonburning carbonate form, which is less injurious to grass, the oxygen content having been dissipated somewhat.

Liming Requirements

Most lawns tolerate a pH range between 5.5–7.0, 6.5 usually preferred. Highly acid soils foster the development of soil fungi, the primary causation of turf diseases. An existing pH 5.5 rating for a medium loam soil (sand-silt-clay) would require 2 tons of ground limestone per acre; pH 5.0, 2.5 tons; pH 4.5, 3 tons. Predominantly sandy (light) soils require less lime and clay (heavy) soils require more lime (than a medium soil) to correct a comparable acidic level. One to two tons of lime per acre (approximately 75 lb/1000 ft^2) generally is sufficient unless soil tests prove otherwise, being disked to a depth of 4–6 in. Lime does not move laterally, and filters downward at a slow rate.

Commercial Fertilizers

Commercial fertilizers are soil additives that enhance vegetative growth and the development of flowers and fruit, containing basic nutrients normally deficient (determined by soil testing). Nitrogen (N), phosphorus (P), and potassium (K) are the primary nutritional ingredients (N-P-K), represented, respectively, as percentages of the total contents purchased (10-6-4, 16-8-8, etc.). The remainder of the ingredients consist of inert matter (essentially sand), the presence of which makes possible a more uniform distribution of the fertilizing materials; also, the filler material helps prevent the bonding, or caking, of the chemical elements while in storage.

The following terms should be understood.

Mixed Fertilizer: Any fertilizer blend of two or more nutritional ingredients.

Complete Fertilizer: A mixture of nitrogen (N), phosphorus (P), and potassium (K).

Fertilizer Grade: Represents the minimum guaranteed percentages of the respective fertilizing ingredients relative to the total weight of the contents purchased. ("Grade" and "analysis" essentially are synonymous terms.)

Fertilizer Ratio: Refers to the proportionate relationships between the fertilizing ingredients. For instance, a 10-5-10 mixture would contain equal amounts of materials supplying nitrogen and potassium (a 1:1 ratio), whereas the relationship between nitrogen or potassium to phosphorus would be 2:1. The overall ratio would be expressed, 2:1:2.

Note: A high grade (analysis) fertilizer, such as 30-30-30, indicates more concentrated quantities of fertilizing ingredients relative to the filler material, but does not reflect a change in quality. A low grade fertilizer, such as 5-5-5, indicates a high percentage of inert matter.

"Organic" fertilizers include animal and/or plant remains in various stages of decomposition. The nitrogen derived from organic matter is slowly released, depending on the rate of decomposition and the level of bacterial activity. "Inorganic," fast-acting nitrogenous fertilizers are manufactured, and must be used with discretion because of their caustic quality. (Native nitrate may be derived from saltpeter, a mineral containing potassium nitrate or sodium nitrate.)

Sewerage sludge is a natural commercial source of organic nitrogen. High concentrations of organic nitrogen can be synthesized from ureaformaldehyde (processed urine and/or blood). Slow-release "urea-form" sources of nitrogen are desirable, containing as much as 38% actual nitrogen. Ammonium nitrate (34% N), a mixture of ammonia gas and nitric acid, and nitrate of soda (16% N), a mixture of sodium and nitrate nitrogen, represent inorganic sources, the latter reacting almost immediately. Water-soluble (inorganic) chemical fertilizers are subject to leaching and must be applied at frequent intervals during the growing season; they should supplement the longer-lasting organic forms.

Available nitrogen manifests itself as a salt, possessing only slight acidic or basic characteristics. Inorganic nitrogenous compounds that dissolve readily may contribute to a high concentration of various cations and/or nitrate anions; the accumulated ions are measured by a "salt index." The higher the salt index (nutrient concentration), the greater the potential for fertilizer burn. An abundance of soil moisture is required to dissipate such concentrations.

A base, or basic, fertilizer (0-20-20, for example) consists of phosphorus and potassium. Phosphorus appears naturally in combination with oxygen, and is slightly acidic. The superphosphate source contains approximately 20% phosphoric acid (P_2O_5), which in turn contains about 44% phosphorus (P). (Technically, the formula P_2O_5 should not be referred to as phosphoric acid, but rather, as phosphorus pentoxide, or simply, phosphate.) Thus, 100 lb of superphosphate yields approximately 9 lb of actual phosphorus ($100 \times 0.20 \times 0.44$). Potassium (K) likewise is not applied to soils in a pure state, but is derived from potash (potassium oxide), which contains 83% potassium. Potassium chloride contains approximately 60% potash (K_2O); potassium sulfate, 50% potash. Therefore, 100 lb of potassium chloride would yield about 50 lb of actual potassium ($100 \times 0.60 \times 0.83$). The formula on the fertilizer tag, 0-20-20, refers to the percentages of phosphoric acid (phosphate) and soluble potash, respectively, rather than the percentages of actual phosphorus and potassium.

Source:	Superphosphate	100 lb	Potassium Chloride	100 lb
	Phosphate (P_2O_5)	20 lb	Potash (K_2O)	60 lb
Nutrient:	Phosphorus (P)	8.8 lb	Potassium (K)	49.8 lb

An application of 20 lb/1000 ft^2 (870 lb/acre) of a 0-20-20 fertilizer would yield 4 lb each of phosphate and potash. The sources containing the fertilizing materials obviously cannot exceed 20 lb. Superphosphate contains 20% phosphate. Thus, 4 lb of phosphate would require 20 lb of superphosphate; any increment of potash-yielding substances would be in excess of the specified weight limit. Higher concentrations of phosphate therefore must be derived from sources yielding a greater percentage of that particular ingredient if used in a mixed fertilizer. Triple superphosphate, produced by treating phosphate rock with phosphoric acid, yields approximately 45% phosphate. Four pounds of phosphate would require only about 9 lb of triple superphosphate, thus allowing a margin (20 lb minus 9) for the incorporation of potash sources. Four pounds of potash require approximately 7 lb of potassium chloride ($4 = 0.60x$; thus, $x = 6.7$). Four pounds of filler material therefore must be added to the mix in order to attain the specified application quantity of 20 lb (9 + 7 + 4 = 20).

The actual amounts of phosphorus resulting from 20 lb of a 0-20-20 mix would be 1.8 lb (20 × 0.20 × 0.44); of potassium, 3.3 lb (20 × 0.20 × 0.83). Phosphorus tends to remain where deposited, and does not leach readily. A practical method of applying base fertilizer to the root zones of seedbeds is to incorporate it with lime, rotovating to a depth of 4–6 in.

Phosphorus and potassium both contribute to root development. While phosphorus becomes a constituent of organic substances (vital to cell formation), potassium essentially remains in solution, serving as a catalyst for various biological functions. Potassium benefits plants prior to periods of stress (drought and/or cold weather); it also increases the tolerance of turfgrass wear on athletic fields and golf courses. Thus, potassium should be applied to grass in proportions equal to nitrogen; phosphorus is of greater significance to plants bearing flowers and/or fruit.

Starter fertilizers recommended for the growing of turf should be complete specialized mixtures containing a minimum of 10% nitrogen, at least 35% of which is derived from water-insoluble organic sources (slow-release). The fertilizer label accordingly shall contain:

Guaranteed Analysis:	
Total Nitrogen	10%
% Ammoniacal Nitrogen	
% Nitrate Nitrogen	
% Water-Insoluble Nitrogen	
Available Phosphoric Acid (P_2O_5)	6%
Soluble Potash (K_2O)	4%

The application of 30 lb/1000 ft^2 (1300 lb/acre) of a 10-6-4 starter fertilizer would yield 3 lb of nitrogen, 1.8 lb of phosphate (0.8 lb phosphorus), and 1.2 lb of potash (1 lb potassium). Approximately 1 lb of nitrogen, or 35% of 3 lb, should be derived from water-insoluble sources, thus requiring 2.6 lb ($1 = 0.38x$; therefore, $x = 2.6$) of urea-form materials. Of the remaining 2 lb of actual nitrogen, 1 lb may be supplied by approximately 3 lb of ammonium nitrate and 1 lb by perhaps 6 lb of nitrate of soda. Therefore, 11.6 lb of nitrogen sources (2.6 + 3 + 6) must be incorporated in the fertilizing mixture. Nine pounds of superphosphate would supply the necessary phosphate ($1.8 = 0.20x$; thus, $x = 9$). Two pounds of potassium chloride would supply 1.2 lb of potash ($1.2 = 0.60x$; thus, $x = 2$). A total of 22.6 lb (11.6 + 9 + 2) of nutritional sources would be required in the fertilizer contents, necessitating an additional 7.4 lb of filler material (22.6 + 7.4 = 30). The above ingredients should be "scratched" into the topsoil at time of seeding.

Most grasses require from 4 to 8 lb of actual nitrogen per year per 1000 ft^2 (plus about 2 lb of phosphorus and perhaps 4 lb of potassium). Table 3.1 indicates when to apply various proportions of the total nitrogen needs. Fertilization generally creates slightly acidic soil reactions. For instance, ammonium sulfate, a carrier of nitrogen, and potassium sulfate lend themselves to acidity; residual traces of sulfur resulting from the manufacture of superphosphate may be a contributing factor. On

TABLE 3.1 Fertilization Schedule

Cool-Season		Warm-Season	
April	½	Late-April	½
September	¼	Mid-June	¼
Early-October	¼	Late-September	¼

the other hand, sodium nitrate and calcium nitrate (also carriers of nitrogen) are somewhat alkaline. Lime routinely is applied to soils in conjunction with the establishment of lawns or the planting of crops, thus neutralizing the acidic qualities of certain fertilizing ingredients. Lime effects nitrogen loss, and therefore even the relatively nonburning carbonate forms should be rotovated or disked into the topsoil about one week prior to the application of starter fertilizers.

Chelation

Iron is the fourth most abundant element in the earth's crust. The presence of iron is essential to the formation of chlorophyll. Iron occurs in highly acidic soil solutions as a free ion. It characteristically combines with other elements to form insoluble compounds, which cannot be taken up by plant roots. In very acid soils (usually below pH 5.0), phosphorus may become "locked" as a constituent of iron (or aluminum) compounds; thus, both iron and phosphorus would be unavailable as nutrients. Various substances known as "iron chelates" may be applied to soils to prevent the bonding of iron with other elements. Also, humus within acidic soils serves to attract the soluble iron and/or aluminum ions, thereby increasing the availability of phosphorus and reducing the build-up of potentially toxic aluminum concentrations. In highly alkaline soils, phosphorus may combine with calcium, and likewise become locked, or fixed, in the soil solution. The alteration of adverse pH factors is essential to effective fertilization.

Green Manuring

Various nutritional elements synthesized by green plants become available to soil organisms such as bacteria and fungi and new plant growth through the process of decomposition, accelerated by slightly acidic soil environments, warm temperatures, and favorable levels of moisture and oxygen. Succulent materials possessing watery tissues decompose more rapidly than mature growth, straw, or sawdust. Certain plants are grown specifically to provide surface protection (cover crops) and/or to supply organic matter to the soil (green-manuring crops).

In the formation of carbohydrates within the plant leaf, and later, proteins, the elements carbon, oxygen, hydrogen, and nitrogen manifest themselves as the primary building units of foodstuffs. As the decomposition of organic remains progresses, varying amounts of carbon, oxygen, and hydrogen are liberated either as carbon dioxide or vaporized moisture. Protein nitrogen, along with carbon, is ingested by various fungi, eventually resulting in the formation of nitrate nitrogen, illustrating again the continual transformation/translocation of chemical compounds. Carbon that is not consumed or liberated as a gas remains as carbonized residue. Decomposition continues until the carbon–nitrogen ratio within the organic matter approximates 10:1. Beyond that point, decomposition may continue, but the carbon–nitrogen ratio remains somewhat constant (10:1).

Plants high in carbon liberate relatively large amounts of carbon (as carbon dioxide) when decomposed, and therefore contribute a smaller percentage of their original contents in the form of residual organic matter as compared to plants high in nitrogen. Straw and leaves, for example, may consist of 80 parts of carbon to 1 part nitrogen (80:1). Obviously, much carbon is lost in the attainment of the 10:1 ratio. On the other hand, nitrogenous plants, such as young legumes (alfalfa, lespedeza, peas, and clover), possess a narrow ratio of perhaps 15:1, and most of the original content remains in the soil as humus when decomposed. Of course, the carbon and nitrogen eventually are depleted through bacterial consumption, leaching, and/or new plant uptake. Legumes are unique in their capacity to absorb atmospheric nitrogen (with the assistance of certain bacteria) and are invaluable to soil management as green-manuring crops.

When soil organisms feed on humus containing large amounts of carbon relative to nitrogen, the nitrogen essentially is depleted before the carbon. As the organisms continue to ingest the remaining carbon, they also ingest soil nitrogen, thus competing with higher plant forms for the soil nitrogen reserves. However, when organic matter contains large amounts of nitrogen, the saprophytic bacteria serve as catalysts through which protein nitrogen exceeding the bacterial requirements is converted to nitrate nitrogen, thereby enhancing soil fertility.

Microscopic soil organisms, then, both help and hinder the build-up of soil nutrition, depending on the carbon–nitrogen ratio of the plants subject to decomposition. Generally, materials containing as much as 30–35 parts of carbon to 1 part nitrogen trigger more bacterial activity than the nitrogen level within the decomposing plant can support; consequently, the "borrowed upon" soil reserves become deficient for the following year, other factors being constant. However, when the carbon level does not exceed a ratio of 17:1, the plant nitrogen is sufficient to support soil organisms and contribute to the build-up of soil ammonia, nitrite nitrogen, and ultimately, nitrate nitrogen. Alfalfa has a ratio of 11.5:1, and therefore is an excellent soil-improving plant material when plowed under.

While the primary purpose of green-manuring crops is to replenish soil nitrogen, cover crops conserve ions as well as retard erosion. The uptake of elements and containment within living plants obviously reduces the loss through leaching of ions that otherwise would have remained in the soil solution. Nitrogen, potassium, calcium, magnesium, and sulfur are the elements that are conserved most as constituents of plants. Phosphorus, of course, does not leach readily, nor does ammonia. In varying amounts, these elements all become available to new crops when the old ones decompose.

Soil Moisture Levels

Light to heavy rainfalls normally supply from 3 to 12 in. or more of moisture to soils. Once the upper levels have become saturated, any excess soil solutions continue filtering downward, eventually reaching the subsurface water table. Also, soils may absorb water from the water table itself by capillary action, thus functioning to maintain moisture levels at or near root zones (Fig. 3.2).

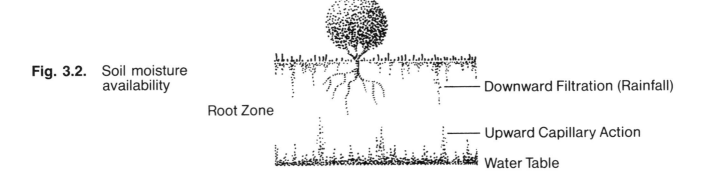

Fig. 3.2. Soil moisture availability

Root Zone

—— Downward Filtration (Rainfall)

—— Upward Capillary Action

Water Table

Mulching

Of course, the water reserves are not inexhaustible, and must be replenished (by artificial means, if necessary). "Mulching" helps conserve soil moisture by reducing surface evaporation. A protective layer of straw is usually applied to newly planted lawn areas, scattered so that perhaps 50% of the seedbed remains visible. Applying 75–90 lb of the weed-free mulching material per 1000 ft^2 (approximately 1.5–2 tons/acre) should be sufficient. Fibrous and solid wood chips, along with peat, pine needles, stones, etc., are commonly used to mulch planting beds, forming a layer 2 in. or more in thickness. The advance of weeds is thwarted by such practices, and the aesthetic value of various mulching materials enhances garden effects. Winter mulching is just as important as summer mulching (in colder climates); plants frozen with an adequate moisture content suffer less damage than when frozen dry.

The decomposition of organic mulches is accomplished essentially by soil organisms that feed on both soil nitrogen and the organic material, as previously explained. Ordinarily, the bacterial ingestion of protein nitrogen from decaying plants tends to replenish the nitrate forms of soil nitrogen that may have been consumed. However, mulches are generally low in nitrogen content; therefore, the balance of soil nitrogen is depleted somewhat when the mulches are decomposed. Fresh straw and sawdust (400:1), for example, contain large amounts of carbon relative to nitrogen, and do not decompose rapidly. Consequently, though quite effective in conserving moisture, the latter contribute greatly to a net loss of nitrate nitrogen essential to plant growth.

Peat, as mentioned, may be applied as a mulch, or it may be incorporated as a soil conditioner, thus increasing the water-, air-, and/or nutrient-holding capacity of earth environments. The semicarbonized, partially decomposed vegetable tissue is derived from bogs (sphagnum peat), marshes (reed or sedge peat), deep waters (seaweed), and the floor of a forest (wood peat and leaf mold). Sphagnum peat is a coarse, fibrous, brown-colored aquatic moss. Common commercial forms are acidic, and therefore recommended for members of the heath family like azaleas and rhododendrons. Certain kinds of sedge peat are not strongly acid, often specified in the greens mix for golf courses. Natural deposits of the mildly acidic organic muck, blackened with age, are found in the glaciated marshlands of Michigan and New York. Almost all forms of peat are satisfactory in conserving soil moisture, though the crusting of surface layers tends to impede rainfall penetration.

Soil cultivation is essential to maximize the productive potential of arable lands over a period of years. Though such specialized practices as crop rotation and contour plowing are the direct concern of agricultural experts, students of land planning and/or environmental design (ornamental horticulture) should understand and appreciate the fundamental processes responsible for sustaining vegetation. The earth's surface reserves must be managed and maintained intelligently so that our physical heritage may continue to be tomorrow's legacy.

4

The Establishment of
Green Spaces

The undulations of the earth's surface manifest a panorama of oceans, rivers, mountains, valleys, plains, deserts, forests, and meadows, each earth form supporting native vegetative species. Our living environment provides a habitat for the coexistence of wildlife and man. The ecological balance of nature and the very survival of humanity depend on wise utilization of our planet's physical reserves, as mentioned in the previous chapter. Wantonly uprooted grasses and shrubs no longer can supply much-needed oxygen to the atmosphere. Earth-binding root systems serve to prevent wasteful washouts, occurring as gullies and deep ravines. Trees indiscriminately cut not only trigger soil erosion, but serve needlessly to displace the nesting ground of forest populations. The channeling of surface drainage and the concurrent protection of plant life are the compelling disciplines of environmental architecture. Sound development practices must stress the preservation of natural land forms; an appreciation for existing surface profiles or contours and native greenery is essential.

The conservation of topsoil and existing plant species is grossly neglected during site clearing and land-shaping operations prior to construction. The sometimes total disregard for vegetative cover is compounded by earth cuts that often are left barren, and thus exposed to the ravages of surface run-off. Quite simply, designing with nature, providing for the retention of significant tree clusters and life-supporting loam, as well as recognizing natural drainage patterns, stabilizes the environment while enhancing the aesthetic aspect of development projects. Furthermore, post-construction landscaping costs are minimized. The preceding chapters have emphasized the fundamental concepts of soil chemistry and plant physiology. In this chapter, the establishment of vegetative cover on sites that have been stripped by construction activities and/or the forces of nature will be discussed.

Testing Soil Structure

The physical and chemical properties of random soil samples should be determined by laboratory analyses. However, casual field observations should enable one to identify surface characteristics of the terrain: When soil is balled in the hand (assuming the sample to be slightly moist), the spheroid may crumble, indicating a predominately coarse-textured sand content, or it may hold its shape, suggesting a silt-clay constituency. The adhesive quality of soil particles increases as the particle size decreases. A light sandy loam, then, is moderately coarse, yet capable of retaining form. A heavy clay loam becomes sticky when moist, and presents a shiny, smooth surface when squeezed between thumb and finger. A medium loam containing not more than 20% clay maintains its shape, does not become sticky, and possesses an intermediate texture.

Another method for testing soil structure involves placing a handful of earth into a glass of water. Coarse sand particles will settle to the bottom of the container, whereas colloidal clay particles will remain suspended in the solution, discoloring the liquid. Sponge-like humus, if present, will tend to float.

Soil Conditioners

Once the existing soil composition has been determined, in addition to the elimination of "wet" areas, soil conditioners may be considered in accordance with the physical analysis. As mentioned in Chapter 3, clay soils are improved by adding sand. A 1- to 2- in. layer of coarse material, spread and rotovated to a depth of several inches, should suffice. The incorporation of ground leaves adds humus and lessens compaction, though lowering the pH level slightly. Lime tends to coagulate clay particles (in addition to neutralizing acidity), thereby establishing greater soil porosity. Sandy soils are improved by incorporating organic matter. Obviously, almost any soil would benefit from the addition of top-quality loam. Whenever one layer of soil is placed on another, the existing soil first should be scarified, or disked, in order to establish a bond between the two layers.

The presence of gravel, in relatively small amounts, benefits clay soils by lessening compaction. However, gravel and sand do not attract and retain soil nutrients, and therefore serve primarily to accommodate subterranean air and water circulation. The clay–humus content is essential for the functioning of bacteria and other soil organisms, acting also as a medium for the exchange and retention of chemical ions. A satisfactory balance of soil components—minerals, microscopic organisms, humus, air, and water—must be achieved for maximum plant growth; the role of each should be clearly understood in order to attain soil management objectives.

Cost often prohibits the widespread use of baled humus, except to condition golf course greens and shrubbery beds. Cover crops should be considered on large development tracts such as industrial and commercial sites, parks, subdivisions, golf course fairways and roughs, and roadway berms, to be plowed under as green-manuring sources of organic matter. Also, prior to disking or plowing, the cover crop serves to retard erosion and curtail dust.

Cover Crops

The planting of buckwheat is recommended for the conditioning of infertile clay soils unfavorable to most other vegetative species. Germinating within six days, the fast-maturing growth should be plowed under when it reaches a height of about 8 in. The planting of several crops is possible within a single season, the last of which normally would be harvested in September. Buckwheat, though associated with the production of honey, affords little green-manuring nutrition, serving instead to improve soil structure.

Winter rye is used extensively as a cover crop, usually sown in early fall, sometimes following the disking of buckwheat. The germination period is seven days. Rye contributes a large amount of organic matter to soils when plowed under in the spring; however, its nitrogen content is not significant. Nonleguminous buckwheat and rye both tolerate acidity.

Hairy vetch is a fall-planted winter annual attaining maturity during late spring. The maximum nitrogen content of legumes is achieved just short of maturity; therefore, to benefit the soil most, the crop should be plowed under during early to mid-May, depending on climatic conditions. The germination period for vetch is 14 days; thus, surface protection may be afforded within two to four weeks. At any time thereafter the crop can, of course, be turned under to increase the humic content of the soil. A pH of 6.5 is desired for the production of hairy vetch, which thrives on most any well-drained terrain.

Soybeans are a summer annual planted in May, maturing in the fall. The germination period is eight days. Soybeans should be plowed under when the beans in the pods are about half grown. A pH of 6.0 is preferable, though a wide range of soils is tolerated.

Sweet clover is a biennial (maturing during the second year of growth), usually planted in early spring. The germination period is ten days, at pH 6.5 or above. Sweet clover adapts to poor soils (which should be corrected somewhat before planting) and is an excellent green-manuring crop, requiring slightly more than 12 months to achieve its maximum nitrogen content.

Alfalfa is one of the most effective green-manuring forms of vegetation. The perennial supplier of nitrogen benefits open fields that may remain undeveloped for lengthy periods. Seeding should be performed in early spring or late summer, on neutral to slightly alkaline, well-drained soil. The germination period is seven days.

Alfalfa depends on certain soil bacteria to obtain its nitrogen content: The bacteria attach themselves to the plant roots and ingest atmospheric nitrogen, some of which is transmitted to the soil and/or the plant itself. The plant in turn feeds the bacteria—a symbiotic relationship involving the living together of two dissimilar organisms. The presence of bacteria creates a swelling of the root, referred to as a node, nodule, or tubercle. The observation of root nodules may or may not indicate the continued presence of desirable bacteria.

Legume seed should be inoculated (treated) with bacteria within two hours prior to planting, thereby assuring the introduction of the required bacteria for a particular crop. Soybeans, unlike alfalfa, will grow without bacterial activity, but, like all legumes, cannot produce soil nitrogen unless bacteria are present.

When cover crops, including sod, are plowed under, nitrogenous fertilizers should be incorporated in the soil to compensate for the bacterial ingestion of both soil and plant nitrogen during the process of decomposition. The full benefit of the green-manuring material is thereby realized. All plowed areas that are to accommodate lawns or other vegetative growth should be disked and leveled. Heavy clay soils on farm land often are left fallow (uncultivated) after fall plowing. The freezing-thawing action of the winter months tends to pulverize the clay masses prior to spring disking and subsequent planting.

Seedbed Preparation for Lawns

Seedbed preparation for lawns begins with the removal of large stones and miscellaneous debris. Building contractors routinely bury bits of plaster, chunks of concrete, metal straps, etc., thus compounding the task of the nurseryman. Subsurface construction refuse hinders root development physically and may alter the soil pH chemically. Calcareous plaster and cement, for instance, would adversely affect an acidic environment favorable to many broad-leaved evergreens.

Drainage problems must be corrected, provisions being made to slope the ground from buildings on all sides (a minimum of $\frac{1}{4}$ in./ft for grassed areas; $\frac{1}{8}$ in./ft for hard surfaces). Whenever possible, naturalistic swales should be gently contoured to carry away excess water. Drop inlets and drainage tubing must be installed where needed. If grading is necessary or desired, all non-green-manuring vegetation within the work limits should be stripped and discarded, followed by the stockpiling of existing topsoil. When the proposed subgrades have been established, all areas to receive the replacement of at least 4 in. of topsoil should be rotovated. After the finish or surface grades have been attained by the placement of topsoil, including any soil-conditioning additives, the seedbed is raked smooth.

As mentioned in Chapter 3, dolomitic limestone contains magnesium, and therefore should be specified for quality lawns. Apply with a Cyclone-type seeder-spreader generally at the rate of 75 lb/1000 ft². Base fertilizers should supply perhaps 2 lb of actual phosphorus and 3–4 lb of potassium per 1000 ft²; thus, 20 lb of 0-20-20 or 25 lb of 0-15-15 would be adequate (in conjunction with starter fertilizer). The lime and base fertilizer should be rotovated or disked into the topsoil, and the surface again raked smooth.

Several days should elapse before applying starter fertilizer and seeding. The interval allows for the dissipation of any highly active liming ingredients. Thoroughly hosing the seedbed at this time reveals water-holding depressions that must, of course, be eliminated. The application of 25 lb of a 10-6-4 specialized turf-type starter fertilizer (per 1000 ft²) usually is sufficient (on a dry surface), thereby yielding 2.5 lb of nitrogen, 0.7 lb of phosphorus, and 0.8 lb of potassium (refer again to Chapter 3). Twenty pounds of 12-12-12, for example, would furnish 2.4 lb of nitrogen, 1 lb of phosphorus, and 2 lb of potassium.

Theoretically, grass requires the primary nutritional elements in proportions approximating a 3:1:2 ratio. Note, however, that nitrogen is susceptible to severe leaching and must be replenished most often. Also, the constant renewal of vegetative growth on well-maintained lawns demands an abundance of readily available soil nitrates. Therefore, the total amount of nitrogen specified in fertilizers on an annual basis may double what the above ratio would indicate, supplemental quantities often being applied exclusive of other elements.

Grass Species

The appropriate seed depends on regional weather patterns and solar exposure. State agricultural research centers at major universities may be consulted for recommendations within a particular locality. Numerous publications are available free of charge. Several complementary grass species often are combined, thereby incorporating the qualities of each, further assuring a successful stand. Certain strains withstand summer heat or winter cold, while others are more resistant to various diseases.

Generally, grasses are classified as "cool-season" or "warm-season." The approximate dividing line extends from Richmond, Virginia, southward along the piedmont of the Blue Ridge Mountains to Atlanta, Georgia, then northward to Lexington, Kentucky, continuing westward to Oklahoma City, Oklahoma, angling to the southwest through northern New Mexico and Arizona, northward again along the mountains of central-eastern California, and, finally, terminating near San Francisco.

Cool-Season Grasses

The following mixes are used for various locations depending on the amount of sun and slope.

Open Sunny Areas

> 30% Common Kentucky Bluegrass
> 30% Merion Bluegrass
> 30% Pennlawn Fescue
> 10% Manhattan Rye
>
> Seeding rate: 3 lb/1000 ft² or 130 lb/acre.

Shade

> 60% Pennlawn Fescue
> 15% Common Kentucky Bluegrass
> 15% Merion Bluegrass
> 10% Manhattan Rye
>
> Seeding rate: Same as above.

Slopes and other trouble spots

> 90% Kentucky 31 Fescue (K-31)
> 10% Common Kentucky Bluegrass
>
> Seeding rate: 5 lb/1000 ft².

Bluegrasses are the most desired cool-season lawn grass, Kentucky varieties predominating. The dense, dark green blades range from fine to medium in texture, having an upright growth habit. The grass spreads by rhizomes, essentially underground horizontal stems. Rhizomes serve to *store* energy and produce roots, whereas roots (extending downward from the rhizomes) *absorb* nutrients and water. Blades emerge from various points or nodes on the top side of the rhizomes. Fall planting is recommended. Germination requires from two to four or more weeks. Mowing height: 1½–3 in.

Common Kentucky bluegrass establishes itself rather slowly and is susceptible to several lawn diseases (leaf spot, dollar spot, Fusarium blight, pythium, powdery mildew, rust, stripe smut, fairy ring, etc.). A healthy specimen demands abundant water and a moderate amount of nitrogen (3–6 lb/1000 ft^2/year). Merion bluegrass requires 4–8 lb of nitrogen, but is more resistant to heat, drought, and leaf spot, though susceptible to Fusarium blight, powdery mildew, rust, and stripe smut; the latter three are manifested by visible fungus growth on the blades. The medium-textured grass contributes to the formation of thatch (a surface build-up of vegetative remains). Merion tolerates usage and relatively close mowing.

Fine fescues are medium-dark green, upright, fine- to medium-textured grasses that thrive in shade, adapting exceptionally well with bluegrasses. They germinate usually within 2 weeks, spreading by short rhizomes and tillers, which are sprouts emerging from the root system. Fine fescues do not form a tightly knit sod, and therefore should be planted in combination with other species. The nitrogen requirement is low, approximately 2 lb. Though somewhat resistant to rust, fine fescues are susceptible to leaf spot, dollar spot, and Fusarium blight, as well as grubs and sod webworms. Pennlawn is a superior strain of creeping red fescue often specified in cool-season lawn mixtures.

Tall fescue is a medium-dark green, upright to slightly prostrate, coarse-textured grass developing deep roots. The disease-resistant species withstands adverse conditions, requires little care, and is preferred on slopes because of its ability to contain soil, thus preventing erosion. It tolerates shade, germinates within 2 weeks, and is adaptable to transition zones where other grasses fail. Kentucky 31 is an ideal meadow grass not requiring close mowing. On banks it may be allowed to grow naturally, maintaining its color for most of the year. Tall fescue tends to clump and usually is planted in pure stands at a heavy rate. The nitrogen need is moderate, 3–6 lb.

Turf-type perennial rye grasses are fine to medium in texture, exhibiting a medium-dark green color comparable to bluegrass. Perennial rye germinates within about five days, spreads by tillers, and forms a dense sod tolerant of tough usage. The improved varieties, such as Manhattan and Pennfine, are compatible with bluegrasses and fine fescues, though not to exceed 25% of the mixture. The mowing tolerance is excellent at a height of about 2 in. Moderate amounts of water are required, along with 3–6 lb of nitrogen per year. Leaf spot and rust may present problems; armyworms and sod webworms can be destructive.

Creeping bent grass is a cool-season species preferred for putting and bowling greens. The medium-dark green, fine-textured blades spread by stolons (aboveground runners) and are extremely aggressive. Penncross bent is most often specified on northern golf courses, though the upright growth habit of 'Cohansey' (propagated by sprigs) is desirable. Bent grass requires constant mowing in order to maintain heights as low as ³⁄₁₆ in. The formation of thatch necessitates occasional verti-cutting (slicing). Frequent watering is required, coupled with 6–10 lb of nitrogen (per 1000 ft²/year). The target of many insects, bent is also susceptible to brown patch and copper spot, in addition to most other lawn diseases.

Planting Cool-Season Grasses

Seed is typically broadcast by hand. Uniform coverage is assured on home lawns and golf course greens by using push-type spreaders, making two passes at right angles. Mechanical culti-packers are employed to distribute and embed seed evenly on large-scale developments. Hydroseeders disperse a mixture of seed, fertilizer, and a paper-based mulch efficiently and economically in a single operation on open spaces; however, the technique is not practical when the application of seed must be controlled, especially around shrubbery beds where the introduction of grass is undesirable.

Planted areas should be rolled lightly, mulched, and watered immediately after seeding, using a fine-spray hand nozzle, care being taken not to wash away seed or disturb the treated surface by dragging the hose. Moisten thoroughly in order to further blend and firm the seed with soil particles, thus initiating the germination process. Daily applications of ¼ in. of water should be provided thereafter. Once the seed has germinated and the tender shoots have anchored themselves to the topsoil, sprinklers may be activated periodically for short durations. The irrigation frequency should be reduced as the grass becomes established, and the amounts of water per application increased, thereby encouraging the roots to penetrate greater depths. Healthy lawns require 1–2 in. of precipitation per week throughout the growing season.

Warm-Season Grasses

The most common warm-season lawn grasses are Bermuda and Zoysia; each should be planted exclusive of the other. Bermuda strains are medium to dark green, having finely textured blades. The drought-tolerant, somewhat disease-resistant species prefers full sunlight, withstanding high temperatures. An aggressive, prostrate growth habit is accomplished by rhizomes and stolons. Microscopic nematodes may attack the root system. Severe matting of the surface stems contributes to excessive thatch. The tightly knit turf, requiring 4–8 lb of nitrogen, sustains heavy traffic at heights of approximately 1 in.

Improved varieties of Bermuda demand attention and are susceptible to brown patch, dollar spot, fairy ring, leaf spot, powdery mildew, and pythium. Tifdwarf, a dense hybrid resistant to nematodes and tolerant of close mowing, is preferred on southern putting surfaces. The nitrogen requirement is high, 8–12 lb. Verti-cutting is recommended monthly during summer weather, followed by light fertilization. Tifton 419 Bermuda is a dense, dark green, somewhat upright, fine-textured grass adaptable to fairways, tees, and residential grounds. The frost-tolerant specimen develops an extensive root system, requiring 3–6 lb of nitrogen per year. Dollar spot is probably the most frequent disease. Damaging aphids, chinch bugs, grubs, mites, worms, etc., may infest any grass species, often being detected only by close scrutiny of the entire lawn environment.

Zoysia forms a dense, dark green, fine to medium turf resistant to weeds. Disease and insect pests are relatively few. The species tolerates heat, drought, salt, sand, and intense wear, requiring moderate amounts of nitrogen. Zoysia establishes rather slowly, responding well to a mowing height of 1 in. or less. The superior strain of southern sod tends to accumulate thatch.

Coarse-textured St. Augustine grass thrives in shade, developing stolons adaptable to almost pure sand. Requiring much water and moderate amounts of nitrogen (4–6 lb), the salt-tolerant specimen prefers a height of about 2 in. Thatch accumulation may be excessive. The species suffers from St. Augustine Decline, a virus extremely difficult to treat. Propagation is by stolonization.

Planting Warm-Season Grasses

Common Bermuda seed may be hulled or unhulled. The seeding rate for hulled is 2 lb/1000 ft^2; unhulled: 5–10 lb/1000 ft^2. The improved varieties of Bermuda grass and Zoysia are established vegetatively from plugs, sprigs, or chopped stolons. Plugs are small clumps of sod, set in individual holes not to exceed 12 in. on-center. Sprigs, or stolons, are short runners of existing grass, placed in furrows and half-covered with soil, allowing the leafage to be exposed. Shredded sprigs often are hand-broadcast at the rate of at least five bushels per 1000 ft^2, and lightly covered with topsoil and/or peat. On large tracts (e.g., golf course greens), the work may be performed with a mechanical planter. Rolling helps firm the root system. Watering is essential.

Seedbed Sterilization

Grasses for golf course greens must be weed-free; often the seedbed is sterilized prior to planting. The process may consist of injecting methyl bromide (a gaseous disinfectant) under polyethylene sheets spread on the soil surface. After being subjected to toxic fumes for a duration of 24–48 hours, the treated area is ventilated for an additional 72 hours. Starter fertilizer then may be applied, followed by seeding and/or stolonization.

To summarize, the establishment of a lawn consists of the following steps.

1. Removal of topsoil if grading is required
2. Grading and scarifying of subsoil
3. Replacement of topsoil to a 4 in. minimum depth
4. Application of lime and base fertilizer
5. Leveling and elimination of water-holding pockets
6. Application of starter fertilizer
7. Hand-raking and/or dragging (mat)
8. Seeding or sprigging
9. Mulching or light top-dressing of seedbed soil on sprigs
10. Watering

Seed Certification

Certified seed must be labeled, showing kind and variety (Merion Kentucky bluegrass, for example), purity (the percent *by weight* of the various ingredients in the seed container), germination (the percent of pure seed that will germinate in a controlled environment), crop (the percent by weight of agricultural, or commercial, crop seed not specified), inert matter (the percent by weight of contents that knowingly will not germinate), weeds (the percent by weight of seeds other than pure or crop seed), and noxious weeds (the number per pound of weed seeds that are extremely competitive and difficult to eliminate). The purity, or quantity, of desirable seed should exceed 90% of the total contents purchased, with a germination percentage of 80 or above. Crop seed and noxious weeds are to be excluded from lawn seed mixtures. Common weeds not designated as "noxious" shall comprise less than 1% of the ingredients. The amount of inert matter (sand, chaff, etc.) should not exceed 3–4%.

Seed varieties vary greatly in the number of seeds per pound:

Penncross bent grass	6,500,000
Common Kentucky bluegrass	2,175,000
Merion Kentucky bluegrass	1,850,000
Fine-textured Bermuda	1,800,000
Creeping red fescue	500,000
Rye grass	230,000
Kentucky 31 fescue	230,000

These approximations indicate a wide discrepancy in the number of individual blades that can be anticipated per pound with each grass species (in conjunction with the germination percentage). Therefore, the seed count is more significant than weight alone on a comparative basis. Generally, the quantities specified should provide a coverage of 20 seeds/in.^{2}, or between two and three million seeds per 1000 ft^2.

Common Lawn Diseases

The visual symptoms of common lawn diseases are briefly described to assist the reader in tentatively identifying turf ailments. Specialists should be consulted to diagnose and treat major disorders. Obviously, lawns also may suffer from improper maintenance procedures, adverse environmental factors, and/or the infestation of pests.

Brown patch severely attacks nitrogenized bent and Bermuda grasses as well as other species in midsummer, following periods of prolonged heat and humidity. The disease typically browns out relatively large, curvilinear configurations having darkened edges. Copper spot appears as the name suggests, affecting individual areas no more than about 3 in. in diameter. Bent grass is the primary target during hot, humid weather. Dollar spot is manifested by bleached areas normally the size of a silver dollar; the well-defined circles may coalesce, thereby creating larger patterns. The symptoms of copper spot and dollar spot can be quite similar, excepting the respective colorations of damaged blades. Circular bands of dark green, often accompanied by the growth of mushrooms, indicate the presence of fairy ring. Eventually, the encircled sod suffers a deficiency of water and nutrients. Organic matter within the soil fosters the development of fairy ring fungi. The invasion of Fusarium blight is signaled by patches of light green a few inches across, later becoming straw-colored. The spreading of the disease ordinarily contaminates sections 1–3 ft in diameter, characterized by a central "frog-eye" tuft of apparently healthy turf.

Leaf spot infests individual grass blades, producing elongated brown spots ringed with dark edges. Powdery mildew also attacks the leaf blade, ultimately covering the entire surface with an accumulation of dust-like fungi. Low light intensities and poor air circulation favor the disease. Heat, high humidity, and inadequate ventilation help promote an invasion of pythium. Sometimes known as "cottony blight" or "grease spot," pythium resembles dollar spot in isolated areas, though the over-all path of destruction is broadly streaked. When lawns are laden with morning dew, areas of infestation often reveal white mycelium (cobweb-like filaments). The peripheral leaves may appear water-soaked, hosting active parasites. Growth-inhibited grass is especially susceptible to rust, a disease transmitted by physical contact. Orange-red-yellow pustules (surface blemishes) are symptomatic. Stripe smut develops from within the leaf blade itself, evidenced by pale yellow veins. Internal pressure eventually ruptures the veins, thus shredding the leaf and exposing dark spores.

A variety of chemicals are available to combat specific lawn diseases. Reputable nurseries and local garden supply outlets should be consulted whenever gardening and lawn maintenance problems arise. However, extensive soil preparation initially and the proper selection of seed, coupled with adequate fertilization and watering schedules, largely determine the longevity of luxurious, disease-free grass.

Damping-off refers to the premature wilting of grass seedlings. The condition can be caused by various fungi, heavy soil, or the crowding of plants. Excessive watering easily drowns young root systems.

Mowing New Lawns

The creeping, ground-hugging stoloniferous types of warm-season grasses develop densely spaced blades, forming a mat-like cover that tolerates close mowing. The nodes (points of blade emergence) of cool-season rhizomes are spaced farther apart, and the upright blades are more elongated. New lawns should be mowed when the grass has exceeded its normal cutting height by approximately 30%. It should be noted that cool-season grasses suffer most from severe cutting, which depletes the blades of energy-producing chloroplasts. During midsummer, extend the normal cutting height of bluegrasses and fescues.

Planting on Slopes

Steep embankments are subject to erosion and/or mass slippage, and, of course, are most difficult to maintain when planted. Tall fescue (K-31) adapts well to slopes, but must be cut on occasion, if only to remove the early-spring and late-fall growth. Crown vetch (*Coronilla varia*), once established, is essentially maintenance-free, while affording white-pink-purple flower colorations throughout the summer. The deep green oval leaflets persist for the remainder of the year.

Crown vetch, a perennial sweet pea-like legume, thrives on almost any soil with a minimum of preparation, as evidenced when rock-exposing earth cuts adjacent to highways are successfully hydro-seeded. Generally, two tons of ground limestone, 500 lb of 0-20-20 fertilizer, and 400 lb of 38-0-0 urea-form nitrogen per acre should be specified. One pound of seed per 1000 ft^2 is quite sufficient, accompanied by 1 lb (40 lb/acre) of either red fescue or Manhattan rye. Seeding may be performed at any time during non-winter months. The seed itself must be inoculated to encourage germination. The materials (including inoculant) can be combined with water in the tank of the hydro-seeder and applied simultaneously. Wood cellulose pulp (200 lb/acre) may be incorporated in the solution to "anchor" the seed when sprayed. Traditionally, mulching materials have consisted of straw (2 tons/acre) and asphalt emulsion, though newly developed plastic emulsions and/or paper-based substances conveniently afford excellent surface protection in lieu of straw.

Planting Trees and Shrubs

Most trees and shrubs thrive best at a pH range satisfactory to grasses (5.5–7.0). Acid-tolerant plants prefer a pH of 5.0–5.5. The pH level can be lowered one digit (say, from pH 6.0 to 5.0) by applying 2 lb of aluminum sulfate per 100 ft^2 on loam soils, 1 lb on sandy soils, or 3 lb on clay soils. Usually the only provision for such plants as azaleas and camellias is to incorporate peat around the root ball; the peat should be soaked thoroughly prior to application. Preferably, the root systems of broad-leaved evergreens should be treated with a water-soluble soil acidifier and plant food, such as Stern's Miracid (30-10-10). The contents also include chelated iron, copper, and zinc. The high nitrogen level and the available iron help prevent the yellowing of leaves. Otherwise, trees and shrubs generally do not require extensive soil preparation, except to be afforded a fair balance between sand and clay. Marginal soils may be improved by mixing several cups of vermiculite with the backfill material in the planting hole. Vermiculite granules (derived from micaceous minerals) are valued for their capacity to absorb moisture and establish porosity in heavy soils.

The fertilization requirements of ornamental trees and shrubs are not as demanding as those for new lawns; ordinary loam soils supply adequate nutrients for established root systems. Nonetheless, occasional applications of fertilizer must be considered to produce healthy plants having a lower mortality rate. Commercial, slow-release fertilizing pellets (lasting six months to two years) may be deposited near the root zone when planting (following manufacturer's suggestions).

Fig. 4.1.   The planting of trees

The planting hole itself must be dug to the depth of the root ball, and twice as wide. The (vertical) sides and (convex) bottom of the pit should be scarified (loosened) so that the growing root system may easily penetrate the existing subsoil. Also, water must not be trapped (allowed to settle) in the planting pocket, thereby flooding-out the oxygen supply. When the hole has been half-filled with backfill material and the plant stabilized (with the top of the root ball protruding slightly above the surrounding surface grade), the fill material should be well-saturated. At this point, the burlap (on "B-B" plants) should be cut back from the top side of the root ball. Apply water again when the planting hole has been leveled and "ringed" with a two-inch mound of topsoil. In lieu of fertilizing pellets, 1 cup (0.5 lb) of 5-10-5 or 8-8-8 may be sprinkled over the area of the root ball of medium-sized shrubs (before watering a second time, as above). For plants below 3 ft in height, apply 0.5 cup; over 8 ft, 2 cups. The area between the stem of the plant and the outer ring of topsoil should be mulched. Staking is essential for trees over 5 ft in height. The trunk of fall-planted deciduous trees should be wrapped for winter protection, thus minimizing the desiccation (drying) of the bark.

Broad-leaved and coniferous evergreen trees should be transplanted when semidormant (fall to early spring). Otherwise, more water is lost through the transpiration of active leaves or needles than the recuperating root system can replenish. Magnolias definitely should be spring-planted; hemlocks tolerate fall planting if given proper care. Evergreen shrubs, if not too large, may be transplanted at any time, but must be watered at least twice per week until established. The application of an antitranspirant ("Wilt-Pruf") is advisable prior to digging. Many deciduous trees and shrubs can be planted at any time other than their flowering period, if well-watered throughout the growing season. However, most oaks should be prepared for transplantation only during the spring prior to leafing so that the damaged roots may recover before the stressful summer months and thus prevent any die-back of the uppermost central stem or leader. Nursery stock that has had time to recover from the initial digging usually is available throughout the year. The root system of container-grown material essentially remains undisturbed during the planting procedure; thus, potted material should be specified, especially during warm periods. When it becomes necessary to dig and "ball" plants (with burlap) prior to transplanting, damaged roots should be pruned. Subsequently, the leafage should be reduced (by pruning) in order to maintain the previous root–leaf balance. One must become familiar with basic plant functions before attempting to modify the structure and/or habitat of vegetative cover.

II

Design Principles and Practices

5

Introduction to Site Planning

"Landscape architecture," "land planning," "site planning," "environmental design," and "landscaping" all connote some form of activity directed toward the arrangement and/or modification of outdoor space for human use and enjoyment. The term "environmental architecture" seems to imply the planning and structuring of man's habitat. The purpose of landscape architectural endeavors is to organize and implement ideas for better living, based on technical data, various design philosophies, and, of course, the functional needs and objectives of a particular client. The shaping and preserving of the external world presupposes the recognition of environmental factors such as wind, rain, sun; an awareness of native soils and existing vegetative species; an understanding of slope analyses; and, certainly, an insight as to the nature of man himself—i.e., his need to compete, to observe, to explore, to meditate, to be a part of and to be apart from society. Projects may range from the selection of incidental group plantings to the preparation of master plans for residential communities, shopping centers, industrial sites, marinas, and/or golf course developments and other recreational facilities involving several hundred acres of land.

The interior designer is concerned primarily with the arrangement of rooms, replete with fixtures, furnishings, and screening devices. The exterior designer or landscape architect similarly refines outdoor areas. The site planning process essentially involves creating space (exterior "rooms") to be allocated for specific functions. The complexity of the planning procedure obviously depends on the variety, or number, of use areas required and the suitability of a given site to accommodate the proposed development. It is often desirable to separate and at least partially conceal adjacent use areas, thereby affording a sense of privacy, mystery, and intrigue. The professional planner thus strives to structure a utilitarian sequence of individualized areas, or spaces, that are aesthetically pleasing.

Whereas partitions define interior space, masses of vegetation and/or surface undulations separate and define space in the landscape. Students of site planning must become familiar with spatial concepts manifested by natural elements. The expanse of a meadow may be bordered by forests; thus, the trees become a "wall." Valleys are defined by mountain ranges. Bodies of water may become physical barriers, dividing one land mass from another. The experienced planner incorporates prominent surface features to demarcate various use areas; geopolitical boundaries and property lines historically have been referenced to, for example, the course of a river.

Classroom Exercise

The following classroom exercise was conceived to acquaint the beginning student with three-dimensional land forms and their employment in delineating spatial patterns:

You have been commissioned to design a seven-acre community park. The southeast property line measures 425 ft; the northeast line, perpendicular to the southeast line, measures 780 ft; the southwest line, parallel to the northeast line, measures 630 ft; the northwest line essentially lies on a north–south axis. The land is level; you are to establish elevated vantage points and visual barriers separating various activity zones by creating earth mounds, ranging up to about 18 ft in height. Vegetation shall be incorporated to define access points and circulatory systems, to screen certain areas, and to accentuate the landscape; such plantings shall consist of evergreen and deciduous trees and shrubs. Pathways are to meander throughout the development. The theme for the park is to be naturalistic.

Open space shall be provided to accommodate a regulation football field (excluding end zones) and a Little-League baseball diamond (overlapping use areas, if desired, since the respective play fields are to be occupied at different times of the year). Also, a "tot-lot" shall be included, encompassing approximately 2000 ft.^{2} Imaginative play apparatus is to be constructed of logs, rope netting, culvert-type tunnels (aboveground), etc. The presence of a botanical garden would benefit those not interested in active recreation. A 20 ft × 30 ft post-and-lintel (picnic) shelter shall be provided on the site for weather protection and general use (possibly including rest room facilities). The main pedestrian access from adjacent housing complexes (the automobile is not to be considered) is located in the center of the northwest property line. A sense of privacy shall pervade the entire site.

Fig. 5.1. Space delineation

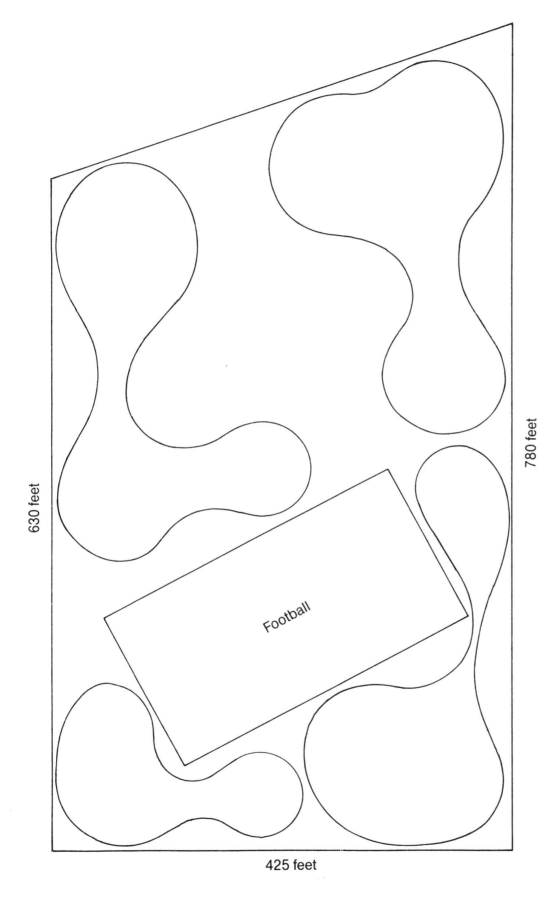

630 feet

780 feet

425 feet

Football

53

An approach in resolving the above is to fabricate a template representing the dimensions of a football field. The rectangular piece of paper then is positioned on a two-dimensional drawing of the property where the designer feels the major play area should be, often on a "trial-and-error" basis. Sport fields should be oriented essentially on a north–south axis so that the sun will not "blind" the players. Once located, the template is outlined on the "base" map, or property survey. Somewhat stylized curvilinear configurations suggesting possible earth mounds are then drawn to provide enclosure and to create spatial concepts, as shown in Fig. 5.1. This procedure is probably the most critical, serving to establish the pattern of development. Figure 5.2 depicts contours and the location of the shelter. (Assuming a 2 ft contour interval, the highest point would register 16 ft in elevation; several "spot" elevations may attain a height of 18 ft.)

Fig. 5.2. The third dimension

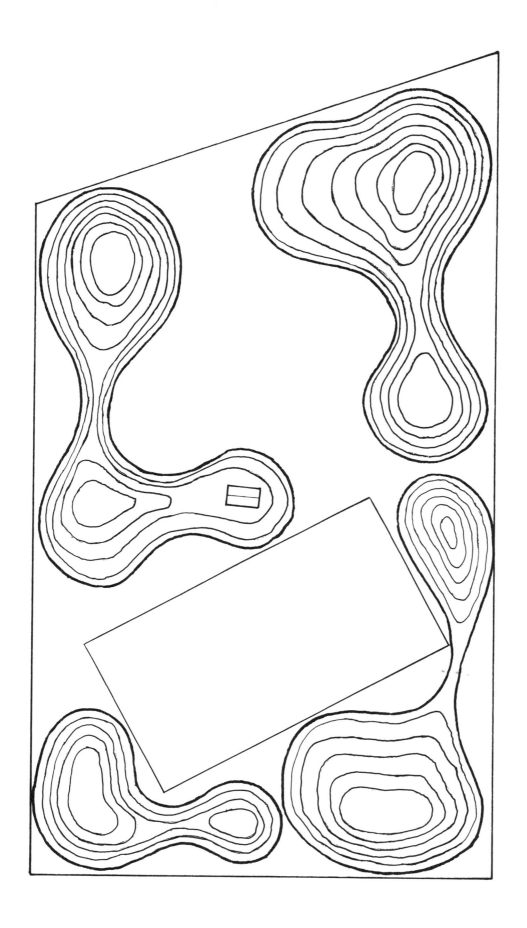

An analysis of the final site plan (Fig. 5.3) reveals that the Little-League diamond has been superimposed in conjunction with the football field. The mound in the southeast corner serves as a backstop for home plate, while affording spectator vantage points. The remaining mounds, coupled with peripheral plantings, in-obtrusively define the property margins, screen objectionable views from the site, and, of course, provide enclosure. The centrally located shelter area, convenient to the tot-lot for parental vigilance, commands perspective of the other major activity zones. The botanical garden is situated relatively close to the main entrance; the sequence of use areas progresses from quietly passive (meditative) to highly active (recreational). Four proposals are shown in Fig 5.4.

Fig. 5.3. A community park

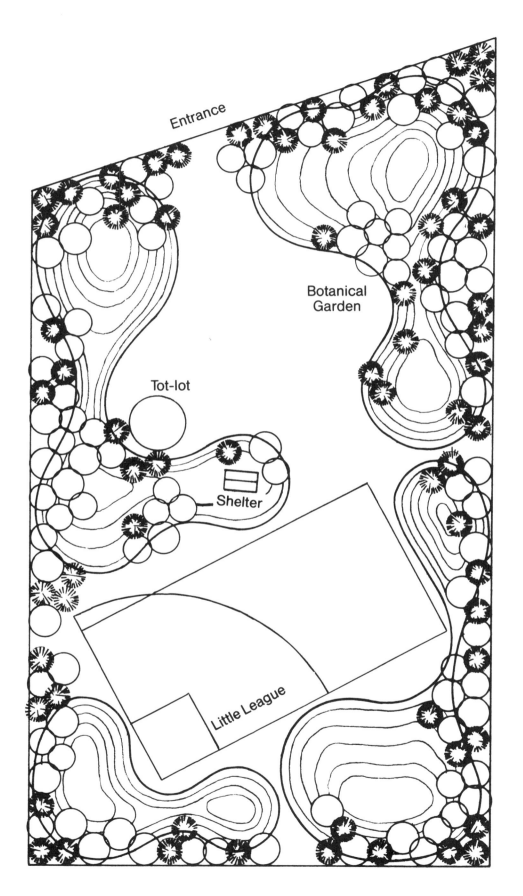

Entrance

Botanical
Garden

Tot-lot

Shelter

Little League

Fig. 5.4. Student project of proposed community park

COURSE: JUNIOR DESIGN
DATE: JANUARY 17, 1974
CONTOUR INTERVAL: 2'

COMMUNITY PARK

INSTRUCTOR: JAMES ROOT
DESIGNER: JEAN B. COX
SCALE: 1"=30'

SCALE 1 - 30

WEST VIRGINIA UNIVERSITY
LANDSCAPE ARCHITECTURE 151
INSTRUCTOR: J. ROOT

COMMUNITY PARK

"Contours" are imaginary lines superimposed over two-dimensional land maps, representing various elevations (in feet) above or below a specific reference point, or plane, commonly sea level (zero elevation). Every point on a given contour is equidistant above or below the fixed reference, referred to as a "bench mark" (for example, the top of an iron stake driven into the ground might serve arbitrarily as "0" elevation). "Spot elevations" refer to the vertical distance of single points above or below the reference plane, falling between contour lines.

The concept of contours perhaps can be visualized by the illustration of an island emerging from the ocean floor to an elevation of, say, 20 ft above sea level. If the "contour interval," or vertical distance between successive contour lines, is assumed to be 2 ft, the third-dimension, or height of the island, may be represented graphically as shown in Fig. 5.5.

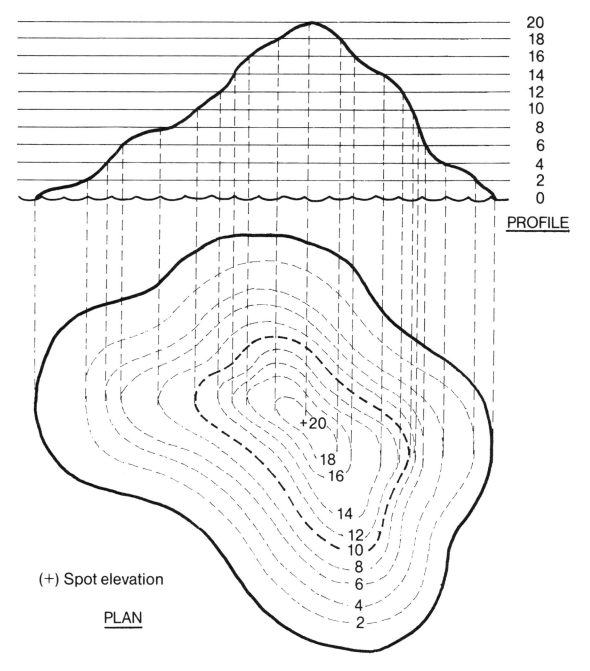

20
18
16
14
12
10
8
6
4
2
0

PROFILE

(+) Spot elevation

PLAN

+20

18
16

14

12
10
8
6
4
2

Fig. 5.5. Contours

A profile simply outlines the vertical dimensions, called "elevations," of land forms, thus projecting a realistic image of the horizon from a single vantage point. The contours of a plan drawing (topographical map) conveniently symbolize the third-dimensional terrain characteristics of an entire area, thus facilitating the consideration of both horizontal and vertical distances in all directions.

The direct relationship between horizontal and vertical measurements enables land planners to calculate the steepness of terrain, and thus determine drainage patterns and building sites. If, for example, a horizontal scale of 1 in. = 10 ft is applied to a contour drawing having a 2 ft contour interval, the gradient or rate of incline can be determined (Fig. 5.6).

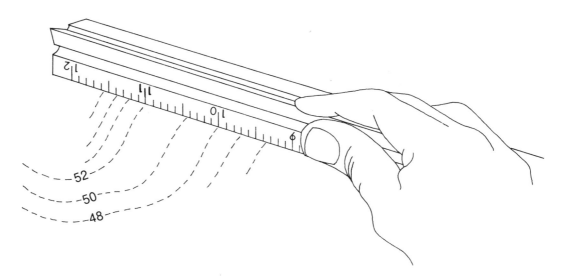

Fig. 5.6. Calculating steepness of terrain

Note: Existing contours prior to site development commonly are shown as dashed lines; proposed contours indicating the relocation of earth quantities are shown as solid lines.

Within the space of 1 in. (a horizontal distance of 10 ft), the contours illustrated represent an elevational increase of 4 ft (from 48 to 52). Horizontal measurements are referred to as "run"; the vertical, "rise." *Rise divided by run equals the percentage slope* (grade). Therefore, this may be expressed: $\frac{4}{10}$ = 0.40, or 40%. A 100% slope exists when rise equals run, represented by a 45° incline (Fig. 5.7).

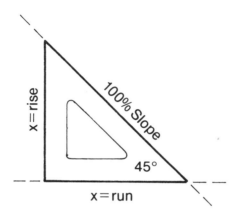

Fig. 5.7. Percentage slope = rise/run

The amount of slope commonly is expressed as the ratio between run and rise. If the run happens to be 3 ft and the rise 1 ft, a 3:1 relationship exists. Thus, various gradients may be expressed as 2:1, 4:1, 8:1, etc. A 100% slope has a 1:1 ratio; 33⅓% slopes may be referred to as 3:1. Usually when slopes exceed 20% (a rise of 20 ft per 100), the "ratio" terminology is used (4:1, etc.).

Roadways should not exceed a slope of 8% for long distances; interstate highways seldom exceed a rise of 3 ft per hundred feet of road. Terrain exceeding 15% generally is too severe for conventional building sites; a minimum slope of 1% (preferably 2% for grassed areas) accommodates surface drainage. An analysis of existing site conditions is essential in determining the feasibility of various development alternatives. Ski slopes and airport landing strips obviously require specific topographical profiles.

Figure 5.8 illustrates the undulations of a relatively large tract (approximately 335 acres), including existing forestation. Such drawings are usually prepared by registered land surveyors. The gradients may be arbitrarily categorized (0–3%, 10–15%, etc.) and depicted by a series of hash marks or other symbols, thereby readily facilitating an interpretation of contour lines at any given location on the topographical survey. The supplemental "slope analysis" (Fig. 5.9) quite simply accentuates the third dimension.

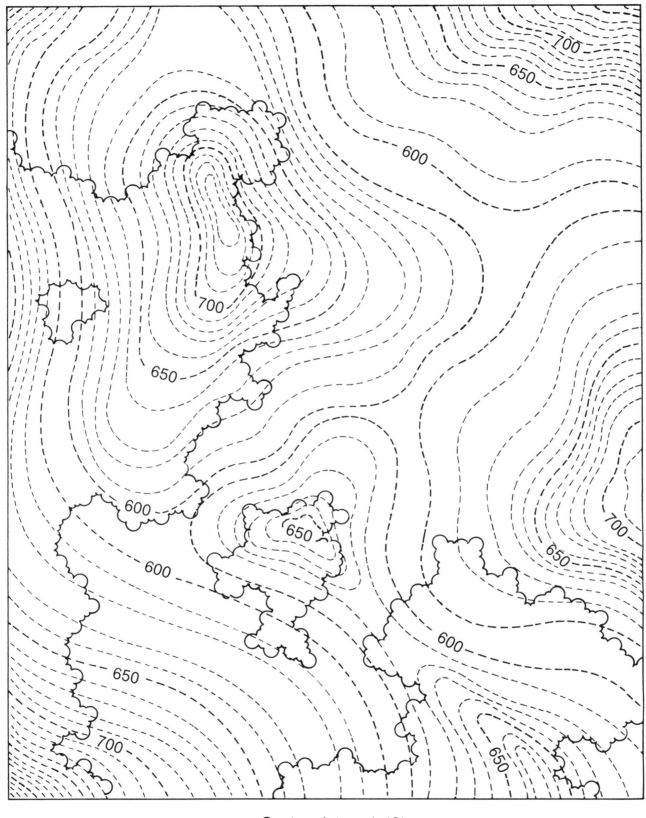

Contour Interval: 10′

Fig. 5.8. Topographical map

Fig. 5.9. Slope analysis

12%+

8-12%

4-8%

0-4%

The Site Planning Process

The first phase of the planning procedure could be captioned, "Research Analysis," referring to the process of defining planning objectives and gathering data relative to those objectives. Information obtained from preliminary investigations may in fact suggest alternate goals, or certainly modifications to the original planning concept. For instance, an analysis of a particular population's age groups might lend support to an additional community swimming pool, as opposed to increased housing for the elderly. The growth of residential subdivisions may indicate the desirability of a regional shopping center; on the other hand, the projected traffic volume thus generated by commercial development might exceed the capacity of existing roadway systems. Zoning laws and regulations obviously bear heavily on planning decisions. The feasibility, or success potential, of an envisioned development program must be supported by an objective analysis of user demand. Cost factors and construction techniques should be examined, based on the completion of similar projects.

On-site inspections of properties obviously enhance an understanding of the natural environment. Taking inventory of existing conditions is necessary to analyze the development potential of a specific site and to correlate proposed functions properly with unique land characteristics. Pertinent information amassed from observations, soil samplings, and research ultimately comprises the "Site Analysis," sometimes referred to as a "Survey Analysis."

Base maps usually reveal property lines, existing contours, drainage patterns—as suggested by the contours—and bodies of water. Significant trees should be indicated, along with the horizontal scale, contour interval, and the northerly orientation. The results of test borings to determine geological substructures and soil types are noted on a print of the appropriate base map, which serves as an in-field work sheet while preparing the site analysis. Panoramic views, unsightly vistas to be screened, "trouble" spots, indigenous vegetation, prevailing winds and seasonal weather patterns, etc., are designated on the site analysis presentation by brief descriptions, charts, and/or bold graphics, usually in color to enhance readability. The recording of access roads, utility easements, and existing land usage lends direction to further development.

The "Land-Use Analysis" phase of site planning refers to the allocation of space for the accommodation of program objectives. "Bubble" diagrams, establishing location priorities for specific activities like housing or recreation, are formulated on tracing paper overlays applied either to the base map, a slope analysis, or the survey analysis. The correlation between the proposed use of an area and the appropriateness of the site manifests the effectiveness of sound land planning practices. Once land areas tentatively have been assigned a particular use, they must be served by vehicular-pedestrian access routes or circulation patterns that are functionally and aesthetically adapted to the terrain.

The arrangement and rearrangement of various land-use overlays produces an organized preliminary plan. At this point the client and the landscape architect discuss relative merits of the "Development Concept," allowing for the incorporation of suggested changes, if any.

The finalized version of the architect's efforts frequently is referred to as the "Comprehensive Master Plan." Detailed construction drawings, known as "working drawings," supplement the master plan, along with additional graphics deemed necessary to convey ideas clearly and precisely. Written specifications usually accompany the working drawings, explaining fully the construction and/or installation procedures to be followed.

The foregoing statements reflect the "methodology" of site planning. Any procedural phase may be emphasized more than others, depending on the nature and scope of specific projects. Also, various steps often are explored concurrently; the findings of one investigation may alter the tentative conclusion(s) of another. For instance, the initial idea to construct an eighteen-hole golf course obviously would be influenced by feasibility studies and the availability of suitable land.

The physical factors comprising the "space" of our planet and the systematic approach in developing land planning concepts are summarized in the *site planning outline:*

I. Spatial Elements of the Earth
   A. Topographical Undulations
      1. Mountains
      2. Moderate to severe slopes
   B. Vegetation
      1. Trees and shrubs
         a. Evergreen
         b. Deciduous
      2. Herbaceous materials
   C. Open Space
      1. Meadow grass
      2. Desert sand
   D. Water
II. Land Planning and Design Procedures
   A. Research Analysis
      1. Program objectives
      2. Feasibility studies
         a. Need
         b. Location
         c. Support facilities
            (1) Existing
            (2) Proposed
         d. Budget

B. Site Analysis
   1. Natural features
      a. Physical characteristics
         (1) Terrain
            (a) Contours
            (b) Soils
         (2) Vegetation
      b. Environmental factors
         (1) Air flow
         (2) Humidity
         (3) Temperature
         (4) Solar exposure
   2. Man-Made features
      a. Architectural structures
      b. Utilities
      c. Roadways
   3. Cultural aspects
      a. History
      b. Present use
      c. Aesthetic quality
C. Land-Use Analysis
   1. Proposed functions
   2. Circulation
      a. Vehicular
      b. Pedestrian
D. Development Concept
   1. Design schematics
   2. Preliminary layout
E. Comprehensive Master Plan
   1. Working drawings
      a. Plant list
      b. Construction details
   2. Specifications

Professional Case Studies

Subdivision Layout

Figure 5.10 illustrates an actual housing development on a 7-acre tract, the building marked "×" having existed prior to the planning procedure. The client requested the accommodation of 16 additional units.

A survey of the site revealed the property to be mostly grassed and devoid of trees (open space). However, the lower elevations bordering the site to the north and northeast were heavily forested; various openings through the canopy of certain deciduous trees permitted the viewing of distant hills. The area to the east had been left fallow. The adjacent property sloping to the northwest exposed unsightly structures, to be screened by coniferous evergreens.

The contours indicate that the highest terrain occupies the central portion of the acreage. The severe slopes to the northeast (below the 970 contour) essentially prohibit residential construction; the area west of the existing structure likewise is not conducive to further development. The well-drained, high ground east of the existing structure and west of the easternmost 980 contour ideally lends itself to the siting of additional housing.

Roadways normally should not occupy ridge lines or the higher elevations of a particular piece of property. Conversely, vehicular traffic should be routed unobtrusively below hillside building sites. It seemed feasible nonetheless to locate the subdivision roadway as shown, occupying the uppermost portion of the tract. Direct accessibility is afforded each lot with a minimum of paving. Also, the curvature of the road is easily negotiable.

An analysis of the plan reveals that the housing units not only relate to each other in an organized fashion, but singly are properly adapted to the terrain; the longer dimension of buildings generally should parallel contours, thereby minimizing any necessary cut and/or fill (grading). The irregular orientation of the units, coupled with judicious plantings, affords optimum viewing and a sense of privacy and individuality for each lot. Furthermore, the property lines are perpendicular to the roadway, thus simplifying staking and maximizing the amount of building space on each parcel; oddly configured sections of land should be avoided whenever possible.

Cul-de-sacs are employed to serve areas otherwise inaccessible by continuous road systems. Such arrangements discourage through traffic, but nonetheless may create congestion if not sufficiently dimensioned; on-street parking should be restricted. The interior nonpaved "island" may accommodate various plantings, thereby screening the nighttime glare of automobile headlights; also, it may be developed as a tot-lot (mini-playground), visible from nearby homes.

Access to the site is provided at two points, theoretically "halving" the volume of vehicular flow at each intersection. The state road abutting the property leads eastward to the population center of the region (Marietta), from whence most arriving traffic would originate.

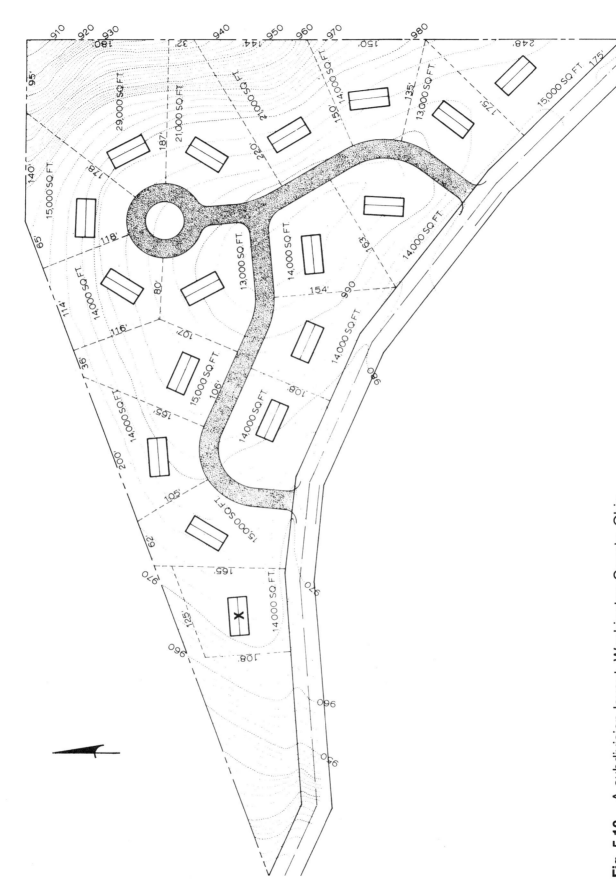

Fig. 5.10. A subdivision layout, Washington County, Ohio

Mobile Home Park

The site for a proposed mobile home park (Fig. 5.11) consisted of moderately undulating terrain, generally sloping toward a central lake. The sparsely wooded area seemed ideal for the accommodation of the intended use; clearing and grading operations would require a minimal amount of disturbance to the natural character of the property.

The client requested that the northern half of the site be planned for immediate development, with provisions for a second phase to proceed southward at a later date. (Quite often developments are programmed in stages in order to generate "cash flow" prior to completion.) The management office was to be situated near the main entrance, just southeast of the first major arterial intersection. The open space to the north and abutting the secondary entrance (between the 636 and 658 contours) had been reserved for recreational activities; at the time of planning, a private hunting club facility occupied that portion of the site.

The community of Davisville is located to the southwest of the site. The state highway department had scheduled a re-routing of Davisville Road northwestward from the proposed main entrance of the park, thereby shortening the distance from Davisville to Route 47, a primary road just north of the site leading to the City of Parkersburg. Parkersburg is located several miles to the northwest of the proposed project. The main entrance thus was located as shown to accommodate a direct access to the eventual linkage with Route 47. The secondary entrance, of course, is located to the northeast, where future traffic would be limited.

The "wagon-wheel" siting concept is twofold: (1) varying alignments afford individuality to each lot, and (2) the utility connections can be conveniently centralized at the hub, or roadway island, of each wheel. Also, the amount of required paving would be minimal. The curvilinear road system throughout the development precluded a monotonous, stereotyped straight-line arrangement of units, perhaps the most objectionable aspect of typical housing tracts. Judicious plantings would provide screening between the clusters of mobile homes as well as adjacent structures.

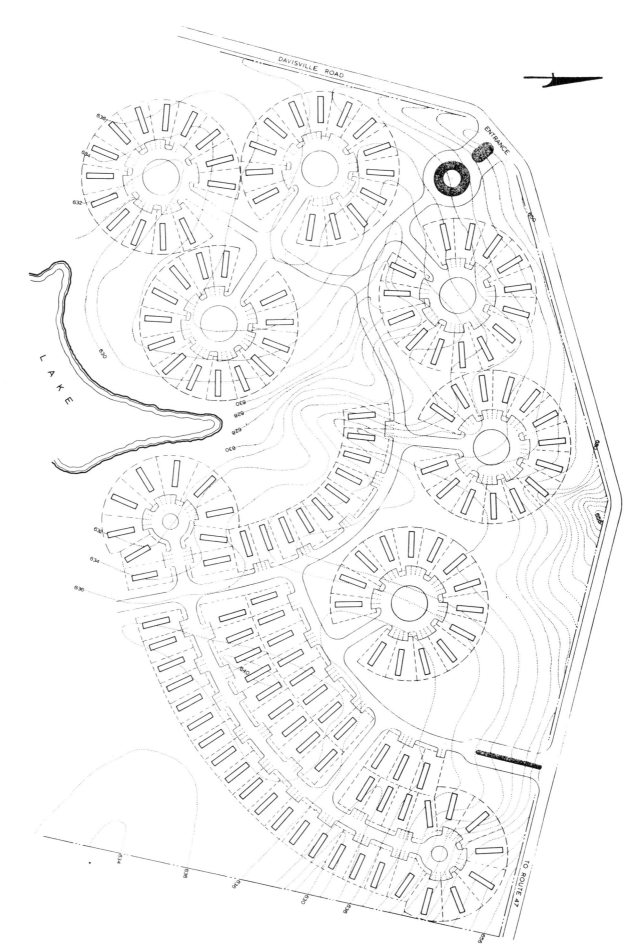

DAVISVILLE ROAD

ENTRANCE

LAKE

TO ROUTE 47

In reviewing this chapter one might conclude that the site or land planning process refers generally to the allocation of space for specific functions, whereas landscaping operations per se are limited to the grading, seeding, and planting of site developments; these tasks normally are performed by nurserymen and landscape contractors. Some landscape practitioners and certainly many clients often are confused by vague terminology. "Landscape architecture" is the generic term that encompasses all phases of land planning and development. The professional landscape architect is skilled in the art of design, and should be retained as a planning consultant, whether the proposed project involves acres of earth moving or simply the detailing of a garden wall.

Fig. 5.11.   Mobile home park

6

Developing the Home Grounds

Selecting Building Sites

Potential building sites vary from wooded to barren and from hilly to flat, each parcel of land exhibiting unique physical features and perhaps differing soil characteristics. Solar intensities and regional weather patterns are significant environmental factors that must be considered when selecting prospective residential properties. Correlating the kind of terrain and the character of the proposed structure(s) is a critical phase of the planning process; architectural concepts should be influenced by and adapted to existing site conditions. So-called traditional homes—Cape Cod, Georgian, French Provincial, and English Tudor, for example—and single-level ranch-type dwellings can be easily adapted to gently rolling to moderate slopes (usually not exceeding 6–8%). Split-level and tri-level forms of contemporary architecture are appropriate for terrain in the 12–15% slope classification (Fig. 6.1A), though parking and vehicular circulation would be somewhat difficult to accommodate without extensive grading considerations.

Frequently a split-level structure is conspicuously sited on flat terrain (Fig. 6.1B), necessitating a series of exterior steps near the entrance. The functional inconvenience, requiring handrails for safety, suggests improper planning; generally, no more than three risers (vertical portion of steps) should be required between the ground level and the threshold of the doorway.

Home builders seldom have unlimited options as to site selection and the subsequent placement or orientation of structures within a given plat. Usually the location for a proposed development is limited to a single parcel of available real estate. Consequently, an architectural style (traditional versus contemporary, ranch versus tri-level, etc.) conceived prior to the site analysis may not harmonize with the terrain. If a suitable site is not available to accommodate a particular structural concept properly, then the architecture itself must, of course, be altered and adapted to the existing contours of the available land. Essentially, the character of the site should dictate the design philosophy; the lines, shapes, and materials of a structure should express the natural setting. Landscape architects are keenly aware of the development potential of various land forms and should be consulted prior to the staking of construction lines so as to assist with design concepts and siting alternatives.

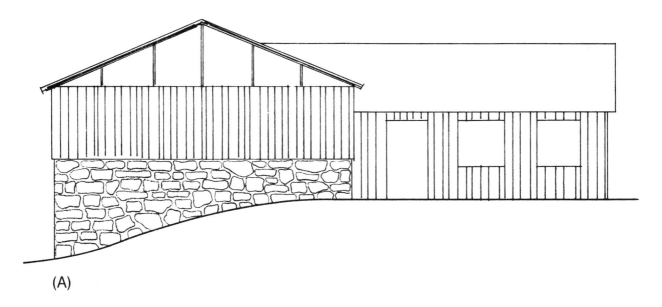

(A)

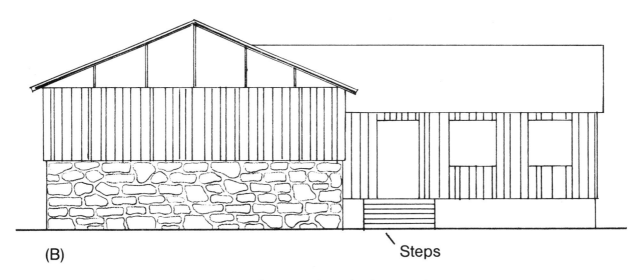

(B)   Steps

Fig. 6.1.   Adapt structure to site. (A) Split-level on sloping terrain—correct
             (B) Split-level on flat terrain—incorrect

Solar Orientation

Physical factors other than contours obviously influence the positioning of housing units. Formidable rock outcroppings, significant vegetative stands, restrictive property and/or building set-back lines, and even the space requirements of a sanitary drain field may necessitate certain modifications to development concepts. The establishment of architectural alignments should be influenced by prevailing winds and the visual character of the environment. The arrangement of rooms may be predicated on extraordinary vistas. The orientation of structures also depends on an understanding of solar positions throughout the year. The Roman architect Vitruvius has written: "The special purposes of different rooms require different exposures suited to convenience and to the quarters of the sky."

Figure 6.2 indicates the sun appearing in the northeast at 5:00 and setting in the northwest at 7:00, angling slightly to the south of the east-west axis at 12:00 noon during midsummer. In midwinter, the sun rises in the southeast at about 7:30, setting in the southwest at 4:30. Accordingly, structures may be sited to maximize the amount of natural sunlight in specific rooms, or to minimize the amount of summer heat penetration. Obviously, not all spaces within a dwelling may benefit from solar exposure as desired. Priorities must be established as to which rooms require more or less sunlight at various hours.

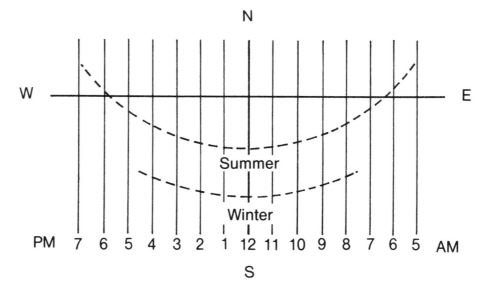

Fig. 6.2. Sun diagram

During midsummer, the arc of the sun is relatively high above the horizon (almost directly overhead). During winter, the arc is much closer to the horizon; the sun rays become more horizontal, less vertical. It should become apparent, then, that a moderate roof overhang would serve to block out the sun during the summer, while permitting the lower-angled (sun) rays of winter to penetrate the interior of rooms having a southern exposure (Fig. 6.3).

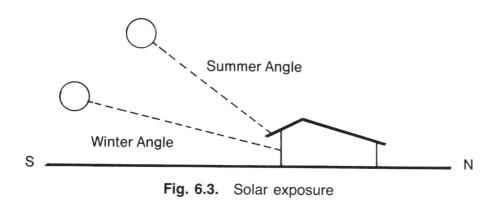

Fig. 6.3. Solar exposure

With the advent of solar heating as a practical source of energy for home consumption, a southern exposure is essential to the performance of solar collector panels. This is to say that a pitched roof containing the panels should not deviate more than 15–20° from a due-south orientation. The following diagrams illustrate the illuminating effects of various southerly exposures (summer solar azimuth) at different hours of the day. In Fig. 6.4 (top) the dwelling faces 30° to the southeast. The morning sun at 7:00 would penetrate the bedrooms and the front elevation of the living room. The kitchen and patio would be shaded. At noon, the sun would affect the south elevation of the front bedroom, both elevations of the living room, and portions of the kitchen. The afternoon-evening sun (fading to the northwest) would illuminate the west elevation of the living room and the entire kitchen-patio area.

In Fig. 6.4 (middle) the residence faces due south. At 7:00 in the morning, the sun would affect a portion of the patio and the east elevation of the bedrooms only. The noon sun would shine directly into the front bedroom and south elevation of the living room. At 5:00, most of the patio and the west elevation of both the kitchen and living room would receive direct natural lighting.

In Fig. 6.4 (bottom) the building is angled 30° to the southwest. The morning sun would affect the entire patio and the north elevation of the kitchen, the north and east elevations of the rear bedroom, and the east elevation of the front bedroom. At noon, possibly the east elevation of the rear bedroom and both elevations of the front bedroom would be illuminated, along with the south elevation of the living room. The afternoon-evening sun would penetrate the south elevation of the front bedroom, the entire living room, the west elevation of the kitchen, and portions of the patio.

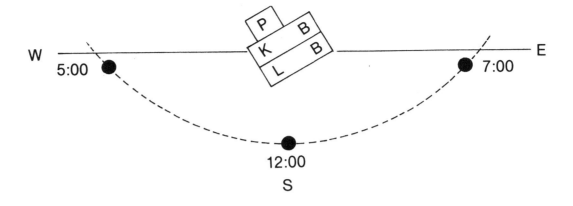

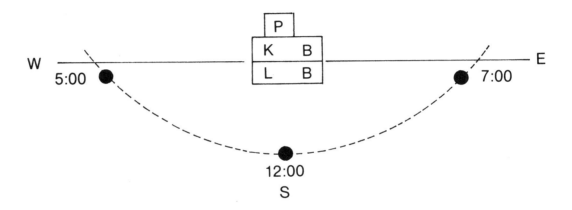

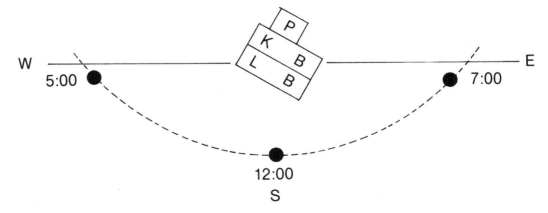

Fig. 6.4. Illuminating effects of summer solar azimuths. B, bedroom; K, kitchen; L, living room; P, patio.

Interior Circulation

The interior circulation pattern of residences should be oriented for privacy and convenience. A desirable floor plan permits isolated access to either the kitchen, the living area, or the bedrooms from a common entry. Also, the foyer itself should be screened from other use areas. Contemporary architects, influenced by Frank Lloyd Wright, often eliminate non-load-bearing wall partitions, thus integrating the space of adjoining rooms. Separation obviously becomes more subtle. Figure 6.5 illustrates an ideal sequence of spatial units.

Ceiling-to-floor exterior glass panels enable the architect to visually incorporate outdoor amenities with the interior setting. The integration of the landscape with the interiorscape psychologically enlarges the dimensions of rooms thus affected, creating a sense of spatial continuity from the indoor use area to the exterior courtyard, patio, or open lawn. Positioning texturally similar plants on either side of the panels further enhances an illusion of uninterrupted space.

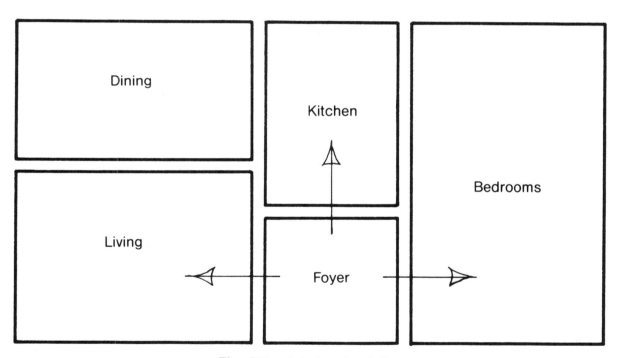

Fig. 6.5. Interior circulation

Landscape architects frequently suggest, and in fact design and detail, modifications to structural facades. Exterior alterations may become necessary to accommodate decks, pergolas, room extensions, etc. The renovation of older buildings obviously entails structural changes. An awareness of construction techniques is essential. Figure 6.6 reveals the basic structural members common to most dwellings.

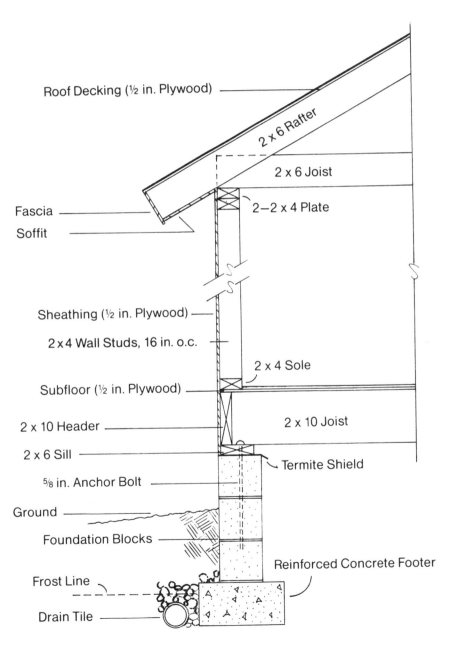

Fig. 6.6. Section showing construction of house outer wall

Drainage Swales

When buildings are situated on slopes, a swale must be provided on the uphill side to intercept any surface run-off, thus protecting the foundations from excessive moisture. In Fig. 6.7 a "reverse" slope is designed to divert drainage from higher elevations. The plan view indicates a 2% grade from the building to the proposed 9.60 spot elevation, and also from that point to the 8.60 elevations on either side of the structure. On-site observations might reveal that a slope of 1¼% (0.0125) from the 8.60 marks to the 8 ft contour may not be sufficient to drain properly the accumulated water as intended. Also, any proposed walkway between the 8 ft and 10 ft contours could further jeopardize the effectiveness of the drainage swale. Consequently, catch basins (drop inlets) should be appropriately located at the 8.60 elevations, thus pocketing the downhill run-off before reaching the flatter portions of the lawn area.

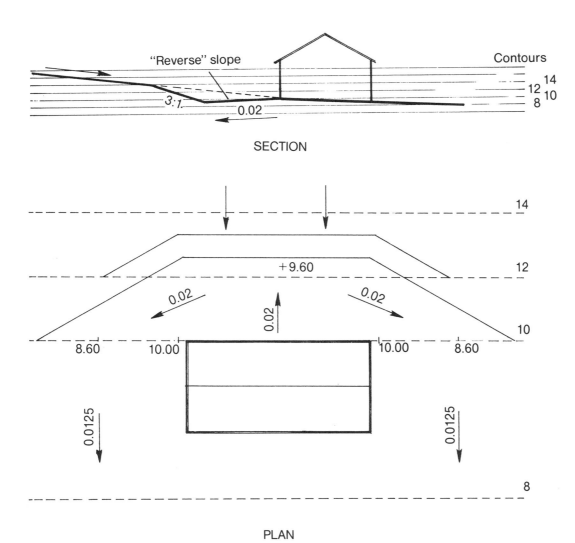

Fig. 6.7. Drainage swale section (*top*) and plan (*bottom*)

Vehicular–Pedestrian Circulation

Once the building alignment has been established, consideration must be given to vehicular–pedestrian circulation. The driveway approach should allow arriving motorists to view the most imposing aspects of the structure. Whether the roadway meanders somewhat or assumes the shortest route between the site access and the parking and/or passenger-discharge zone depends on the distance involved, the amount of gradient, and the architectural character of the residence. Traditionally, formal buildings are approached directly from the front or from either side (horseshoe effect) (Fig. 6.8). The width of a single lane should be 11 ft; to allow for passing, 16 ft. The width of a driveway in front of an entrance landing should be at least 20 ft, thus permitting the parking of an automobile without obstructing the through circulation of other vehicles.

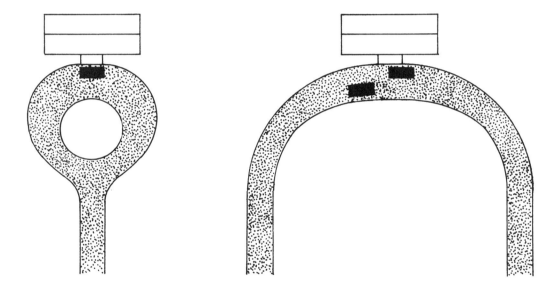

Fig. 6.8. Formal driveway approaches

For convenience and safety, drivers must never be forced to back onto streets. A turnaround adjacent to the garage should be provided (Fig. 6.9).

A landing, or receiving area, serves to welcome guests as well as create a visually strong transition from the driveway to walkway. The width of landings should accommodate the opening of a car door while permitting passengers to step conveniently onto a hard surface; likewise, a person standing on the landing should be able to open a door without having to step back onto the lawn or planting bed. The length should be proportioned to the width, but certainly sufficient to accommodate the opening of both front and rear doors simultaneously (Fig. 6.10).

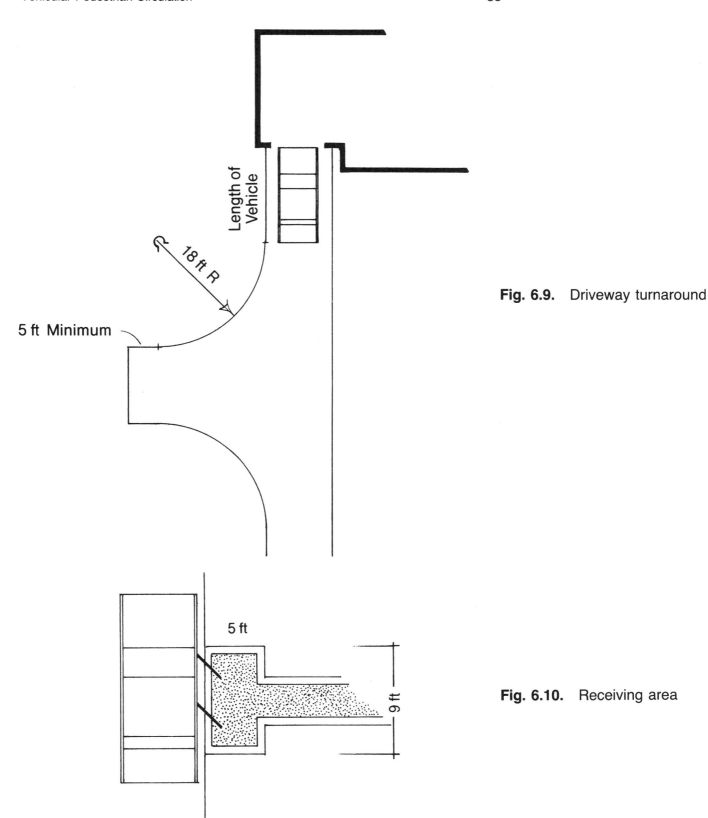

Fig. 6.9. Driveway turnaround

Fig. 6.10. Receiving area

Perhaps the most common failure in residential planning is not providing a vehicular turnaround, coupled with inadequate walks. Figure 6.11 illustrates a typical ("before") concept that easily could be corrected ("after"). The turnaround space in the "after" illustration below may serve to accommodate off-driveway parking. Of course, such "parking bays" normally are widened for two or more vehicles.

Sometimes residences are situated fairly close to property lines, for various reasons, thereby preventing the construction of turnarounds illustrated thus far. In this case, proposed turnarounds can be "flipped" to the opposite side of the driveway, as shown in Fig. 6.13. Also, on a narrow lot, the dwelling may be angled, thus permitting a fully functional driveway treatment, along with greater possibilities for creative landscaping effects (Fig. 6.14).

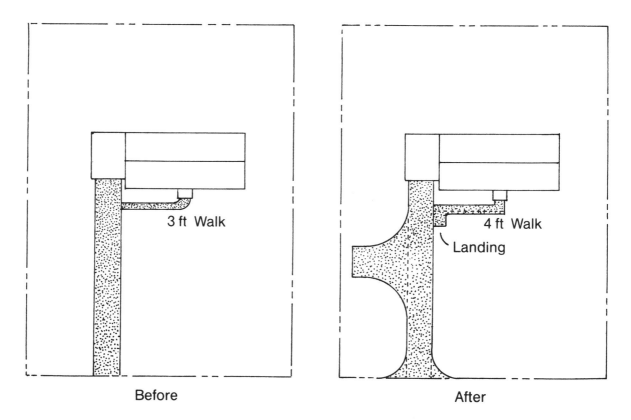

Before   After

Fig. 6.11. Correcting improper vehicular–pedestrian circulation

Fig. 6.12. Parking area curbing using pressure-treated pole sections on-end.

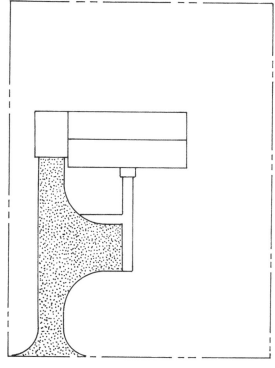

Fig. 6.13. "Flip-flop" turnaround

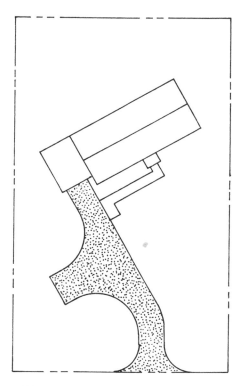

Fig. 6.14. Angled orientation

Figure 6.15 illustrates a unique driveway approach, aligned as the terminus of an existing farm lane. A major consideration involved providing vehicular access to the front entrance without the roadway itself encroaching on the living room side of the residence, thereby preserving the naturalistic quality of the front window exposure. The angle of the entrance walk serves to relate the off-centered access with the front door; the arrangement is intended to divert vehicular–pedestrian activity from living room viewing. The isolation of the circulatory system is further enhanced by the screening effect of proposed plantings between the entranceway and the front (living room) window. Note that the garage access has been provided with a turnaround.

Walks, landings, patios, pools, and retaining (seat) walls are typical architectural features that should be planned and programmed for construction in conjunction with the earth-moving activities related to the erection of buildings and the installation of roadways (Figs. 6.16, 6.17, and 6.21). The balancing of excavation cuts and fills obviously eliminates the need to transport off-site earth materials. A considerable amount of useful topsoil can be salvaged from the site preparation for driveways and walkways alone.

Fig. 6.15. Driveway approach

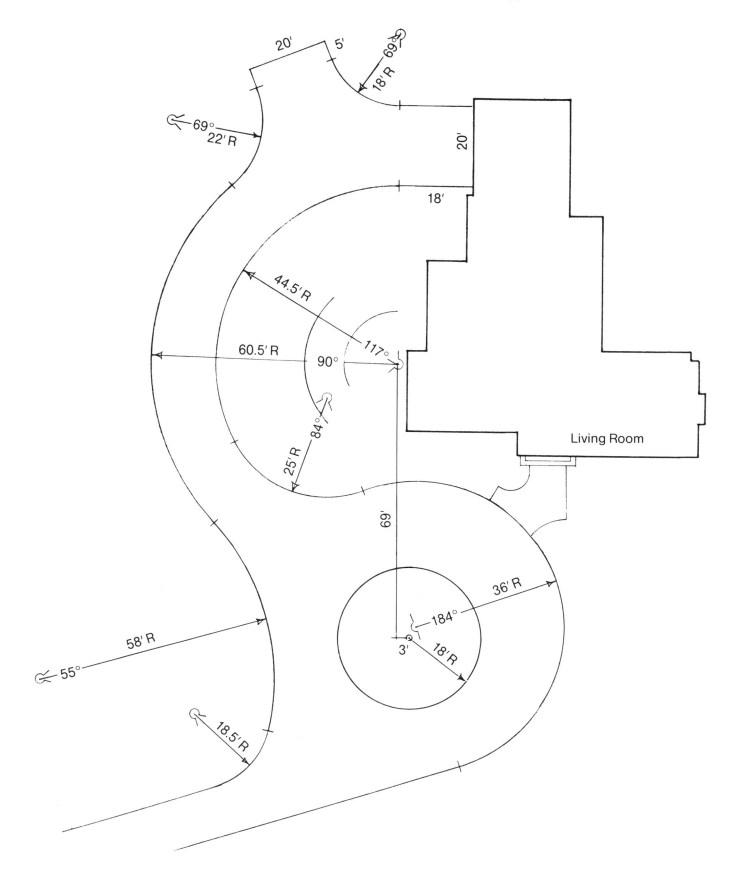

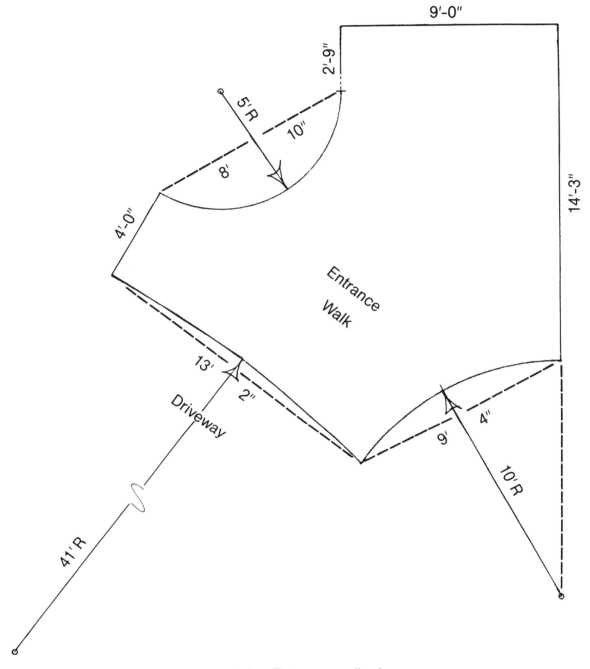

Fig. 6.16. Entrance walk plan

Fig. 6.17.   Entrance walk

Fig. 6.18. Typical walk section

Redwood dividers or other expansion
material, 8 ft. o.c. max.   4 in. reinforced concrete

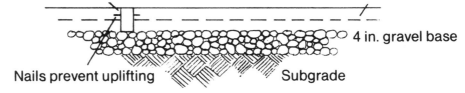

Nails prevent uplifting   Subgrade

4 in. gravel base

Grade stakes indicate the proposed surface or finish elevations and the depth of subgrades for architectural items, as well as lawn contours. Concrete walks and patios, for example, normally are 4 in. thick, reinforced with ⅛ in. wire mesh arranged in 6 in. grids (6 × 6 No. 10). An additional 4 in. should be allowed for a gravel base when the landscape paving is underlain by clay, thus permitting the drainage of subsurface water (Figs. 6.18 and 6.19). An accumulation of moisture beneath concrete structures increases the probability of surface cracking due to the upheaval of frozen subsoil in winter and the eventual settlement from thawing in spring.

Fig. 6.19. Reinforced concrete walk/gravel base

Retaining Walls

Earth cuts necessitating structural support generally should be avoided. Retaining walls are employed to contain embankments when the horizontal distance is not sufficient to accommodate a naturalistic slope. When a gradient exceeding 1:1 (45°) is encountered, several stabilizing options may be exercised, depending on the space restrictions, soil structure, and aesthetics (Fig. 6.20).

The rip-rap method of containing soil and controlling erosion simply consists of placing rocks one atop another from the base of a slope upward. Polyethylene sheets spread beneath the rocks on the soil surface retard the emergence of weeds. Planting pockets may be interspersed, with various forms of prostrate juniper and cotoneaster adapting quite well.

Railroad ties placed on-end are aesthetically pleasing, structurally sound, and weather-resistant. The use of a trenching machine is advisable during installation to control the proper width of the trench without unnecessarily disturbing the lateral slopes. The gravel backing permits the escape of subsurface water, and lessens soil pressure against the wooden members. Approximately 30% of the tie length should extend below-grade.

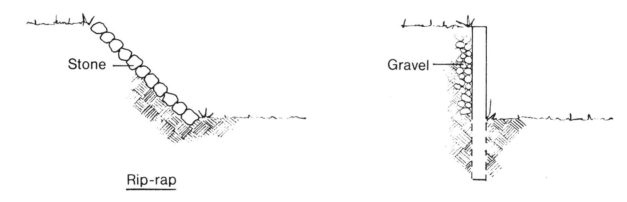

Stone

Rip-rap

Gravel

Railroad Ties

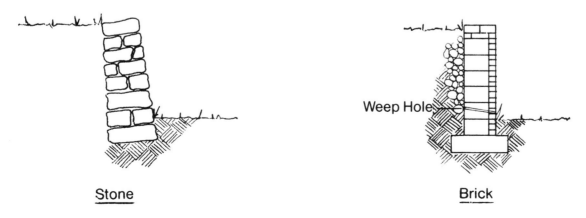

Stone

Weep Hole

Brick

Fig. 6.20. Retaining walls

Local field stone can be stacked dry (without mortar) up to perhaps 4 ft, but should slope 1 in. per vertical foot against the embankment, as illustrated in Fig. 6.20; also, the base should exceed the cap in width. The naturalness of stone enhances any landscaping project.

The brick retaining wall in Fig. 6.20 is constructed with 8 in. × 12 in. × 16 in. concrete blocks, faced with stretcher courses; the cap consists of rowlocks (bricks placed on-edge). Alternative copings might include formed concrete or cut stone. The 16 in.-wide wall should be reinforced with vertical rods embedded in the concrete footer, likewise reinforced. Weep holes and gravel backing accommodate drainage. The bricks should be compatible in appearance with those of adjacent structures (Fig. 6.21).

The sequence of residential land development activities normally includes:

1. Site Selection
2. Building Design and Orientation (interior and exterior)
3. Vehicular-Pedestrian Circulation
4. Site Clearing and Grading
5. Architectural Construction, including roadways, walks, walls, patios, pools, fountains
6. Planting Design and Seedbed Preparation

Fig. 6.21. Brick and block seat-retaining wall

Soil Stabilization

The installation of lawns (described in Chapter 4) usually precedes the planting of trees and shrubs. Seeding operations often are performed by the building contractor as a matter of expedience to stabilize recently disturbed soil and/or simply to improve the marketability of the property. Nonetheless, the proper tilling of the seedbed and the incorporation of seeding ingredients should be the responsibility of qualified lawn personnel. Proposed planting areas in the vicinity of the seedbed should be protected from the dispersal of seed; unwanted grass is extremely difficult to eliminate, once established.

Moderate-to-severe slopes must be given immediate attention. Annual rye often is applied for fast-germination, but is not recommended as a companion to more permanent (perennial) grass species. Heaths and heathers adapt well to embankments receiving full sunlight, requiring a minimum of soil preparation and maintenance. A variety of evergreen specimens have proved to be exceptionally hardy and versatile; colorful drifts of the acid-tolerant materials blend aesthetically with most any garden scheme.

Planting Design Concepts

Traditionally, vegetative masses at the corners of buildings and adjoining the main entrance have been emphasized (Fig. 6.22; see also Chapter 7). The plants should manifest visual strength throughout the year, and therefore must consist of evergreen varieties. In temperate-to-warm climates, the dominant corner plants may include Burford hollies or boxwoods, flanked by smaller Japanese hollies (*Ilex crenata* 'rotundifolia'). The shrubs flanking the entrance usually are maintained slightly smaller than the larger of the corner plants, depending upon the architectural treatment of the entranceway itself (shrubs should not overpower the aesthetics of well-proportioned facades). Entrance plantings may consist of Burford hollies or boxwoods, fronted by smaller Japanese hollies or dwarf mugho pines; rotundifolias faced with *Ilex crenata* 'helleri' would also be appropriate. Generally, scale, proportion, and texture give rise to the selection of a particular plant species.

Fig. 6.22.   Dominant evergreen shrubbery

Corner plants serve primarily to enframe structures. Also, they tend to "soften" the angular projection of the intersecting elevations. The strength of corner shrubs is enhanced by placing the larger outside plant at a 45° angle to the corner of the building (Fig. 6.23).

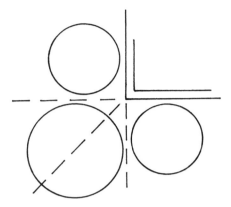

Fig. 6.23. Corner planting

In viewing the residence in Fig. 6.22 a conspicuous void appears in the right-front elevation. An espaliered plant, a large shrub, or a small tree would serve to fill the exterior wall space between the fourth and fifth front windows (from left to right). Intermediate "filler" plants, perhaps consisting of deciduous varieties of flowering specimens, would be appropriate under the windows, not to exceed the height of the sills at maturity. Thus, the dominant evergreen plantings, an occasional espaliered specimen, and a limited variety of filler plants comprise so-called "foundation" plantings, normally extending entirely around structures (Fig. 6.24).

The plan shown in Fig. 6.25 indicates more clearly the positioning of shrubbery discussed thus far. The assigned numbers merely suggest the kinds of plants one might consider for the respective locations.

Fig. 6.24. Completed foundation planting

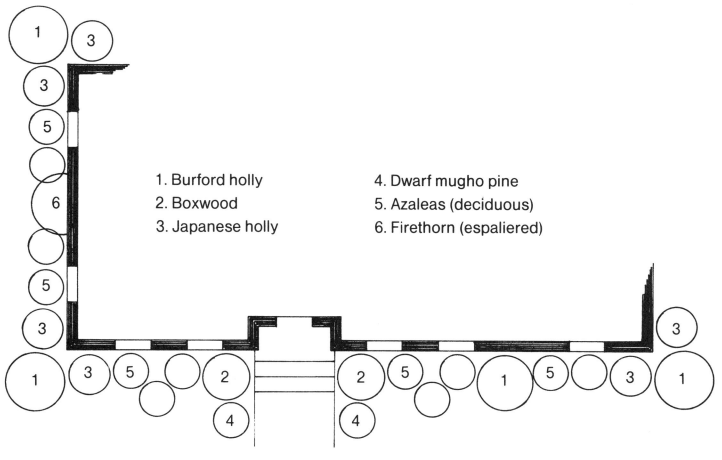

1. Burford holly
2. Boxwood
3. Japanese holly

4. Dwarf mugho pine
5. Azaleas (deciduous)
6. Firethorn (espaliered)

Fig. 6.25. Foundation planting plan

The delineation of planting beds contributes considerably to the overall effect of planting arrangements; most visual impressions are registered at ground and eye levels. The outward limits of the beds obviously must extend beyond the circumference of the respective shrubs therein. To continue with the previous planting concept, Fig. 6.26 illustrates the employment of a reverse curve, always appropriate and effective in the landscape. Natural objects like boulders enhance plantings as well (Fig. 6.27).

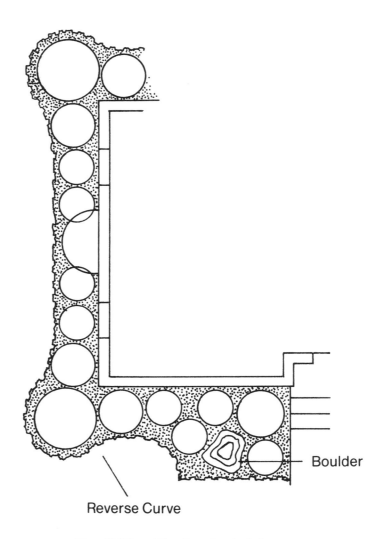

Fig. 6.26.   Planting bed delineation

Fig. 6.27. Use of boulders in the landscape

Many contemporary styles of architecture do not require foundation planting in the traditional sense; rather, a grouping of well-chosen specimens judiciously positioned to complement a particular elevation (of the building) at a single point is sufficient, as shown in Fig. 6.28.

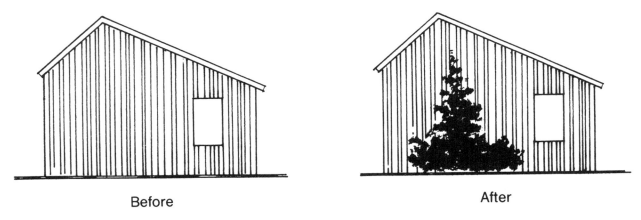

Before   After

Fig. 6.28. "Spot" planting

The following residential landscape development plans emphasize various planting concepts, along with the detailing of fencing. retaining walls, patios, pools, and the dimensioning of driveway turnarounds. Also, a landing detail and the height of a post lantern are illustrated. Generally, the planting beds are curvilinear, suggesting the free-form character of the natural environment. The scale of landscape architectural features in home planning must relate to the human figure, just as various plant species must adapt to their function and location.

PLANT LIST

CODE	QUAN.	BOTANICAL NAME	COMMON NAME	SIZE	ROOT
A	1	ACER RUBRUM	RED MAPLE	10-12'	B-B
B₁	17	AZALEA (RED)	AZALEA	15-18'	CAN
B	16	AZALEA (WHITE)	AZALEA	15-18'	CAN
C	1	CORNUS ALBA SIBERICA	SIBERIAN DOGWOOD	6'	B-B
D	1	CORNUS FLORIDA	WHITE FLOWERING DOGWOOD	6'	B-B
E	1	CORNUS FLORIDA RUBRA	PINK DOGWOOD	6'	B-B
F	1500 b	CORONILLA VARIA	CROWNVETCH		SEED
G	3	COTONEASTER APICULATA	CRANBERRY COTONEASTER	15-18'	CAN
H	13	COTONEASTER DIVARICATA	SPREADING COTONEASTER	3-4'	B-B
I	3	CRATAEGUS PHAENOPYRUM	WASHINGTON HAWTHORN	8-10'	B-B
J	5	EUONYMUS PATENS 'MANHATTAN'	MANHATTAN EUONYMUS	3'	CAN
K₁	5	EXBURY AZALEA (RED)	EXBURY AZALEA	2-3'	CAN
K	2	EXBURY AZALEA (YELLOW)	EXBURY AZALEA	2-3'	CAN
L	1	FRAXINUS PENNSYLVANICA LANCEOLATA	GREEN ASH	10-12'	B-B
M	5	HYDRANGEA ARBORESCENS GRANDIFLORA	SNOW HILL HYDRANGEA	18-24"	CAN
N	7	HYDRANGEA QUERCIFOLIA	OAK LEAF HYDRANGEA	18-24"	CAN
O	5	ILEX CRENATA 'HELLERI'	HELLER HOLLY	15-18'	CAN
P	7	ILEX CRENATA ROTUNDIFOLIA	JAPANESE HOLLY	3'	B-B
Q	12	JUNIPERUS CHINENSIS PFITZERIANA	PFITZER JUNIPER	2-3'	B-B
R	4	MAGNOLIA VIRGINIANA	SWEET BAY MAGNOLIA	6-8'	B-B
S	2	PICEA ABIES	NORWAY SPRUCE	10-12'	B-B
T	6	PINUS MUGHO MUGHUS	MUGHO PINE	18-24"	CAN
U	10	PINUS STROBUS	EASTERN WHITE PINE	10-12'	B-B
V	10	PYRACANTHA COCCINEA LALANDI	FIRETHORN	2-3'	CAN
W	3	QUERCUS PALUSTRIS	PIN OAK	10-12'	B-B
X	11	RHODODENDRON (RED)	RHODODENDRON	18-24"	CAN
X₁	5	RHODODENDRON (WHITE)	RHODODENDRON	18-24"	CAN
Y	9	TSUGA CANADENSIS	CANADIAN HEMLOCK	6'	B-B
Z	1000	VINCA MINOR	PERIWINKLE	6"	B-B

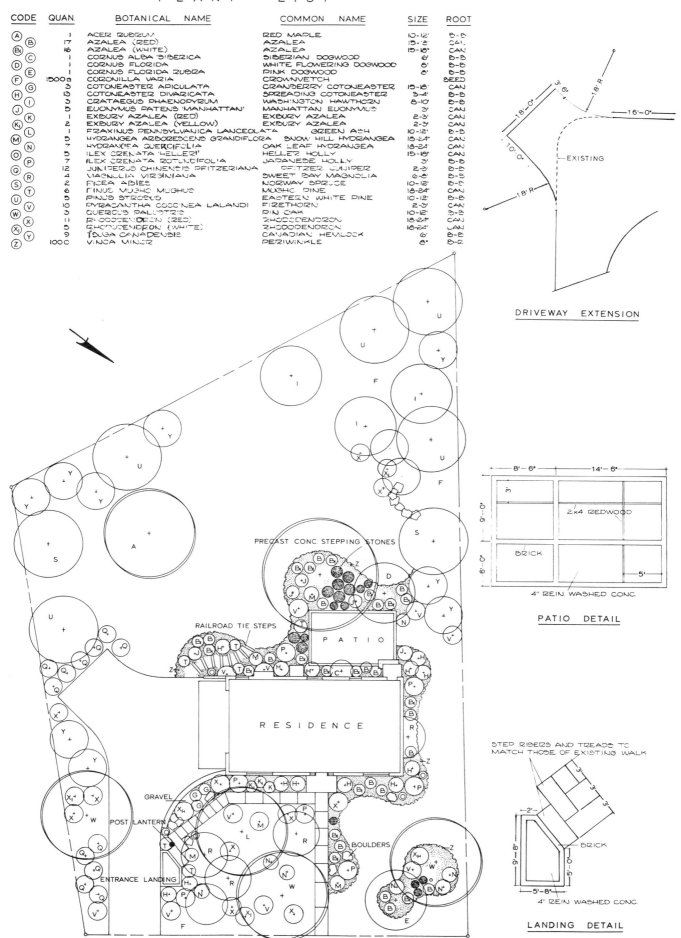

DRIVEWAY EXTENSION

PATIO DETAIL

LANDING DETAIL

247 NORTH HILLS DRIVE

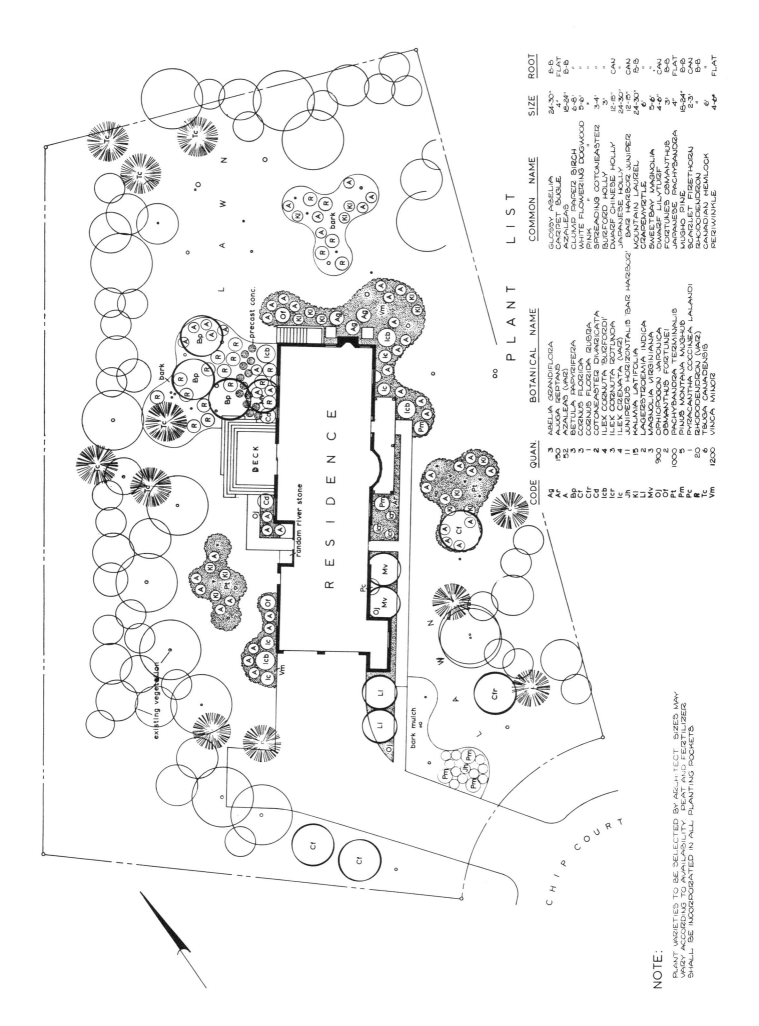

PLANT LIST

CODE	QUAN.	BOTANICAL NAME	COMMON NAME	SIZE	ROOT
Ag	3	ABELIA GRANDIFLORA	GLOSSY ABELIA	24-30"	B-B
Ar	150	AJUGA REPTANS	CARPET BUGLE	4"	FLAT
A	52	AZALEAS (VAR)	AZALEAS	18-24"	B-B
Bp	3	BETULA PAPYRIFERA	CLUMP PAPER BIRCH	6-8'	"
Cf	7	CORNUS FLORIDA	WHITE FLOWERING DOGWOOD	5-6'	"
Cfr	2	CORNUS FLORIDA RUBRA	PINK	3-4'	"
Cd	4	COTONEASTER DIVARICATA	SPREADING COTONEASTER	3'	"
Icb	4	ILEX CORNUTA 'BURFORDI'	BURFORD HOLLY	12-15"	CAN
Icr	3	ILEX CORNUTA ROTUNDA	DWARF CHINESE HOLLY	3'	"
Ic	11	ILEX CRENATA (VAR)	JAPANESE HOLLY	12-15"	CAN
Jh	11	JUNIPERUS HORIZONTALIS (BAR HARBOR)	BAR HARBOR JUNIPER	24-30"	B-B
Kl	15	KALMIA LATIFOLIA	MOUNTAIN LAUREL	24-30"	CAN
Li	2	LAGERSTROEMIA INDICA	CRAPEMYRTLE	6'	"
Mv	2	MAGNOLIA VIRGINIANA	SWEETBAY MAGNOLIA	5-6'	CAN
Oj	900	OPHIOPOGON JAPONICA	DWARF LILYTURF	4-6"	"
Of	2	OSMANTHUS FORTUNEI	FORTUNES OSMANTHUS	3'	CAN
Pt	1000	PACHYSANDRA TERMINALIS	JAPANESE PACHYSANDRA	4"	FLAT
Pm	5	PINUS MONTANA MUGHUS	MUGHO PINE	18-24"	B-B
Pc	20	PYRACANTHA COCCINEA LALANDI	SCARLET FIRETHORN	2-3'	CAN
R	10	RHODODENDRON (VAR)	RHODODENDRON	2-3'	B-B
Tc	6	TSUGA CANADENSIS	CANADIAN HEMLOCK	6'	B-B
Vm	1200	VINCA MINOR	PERIWINKLE	4-6"	FLAT

NOTE:
PLANT VARIETIES TO BE SELECTED BY ARCHITECT. SIZES MAY VARY ACCORDING TO AVAILABILITY. PEAT AND FERTILIZER SHALL BE INCORPORATED IN ALL PLANTING POCKETS.

RESIDENCE

DECK

LAWN

CHIP COURT

precast conc.

random river stone

bark

bark mulch

existing vegetation

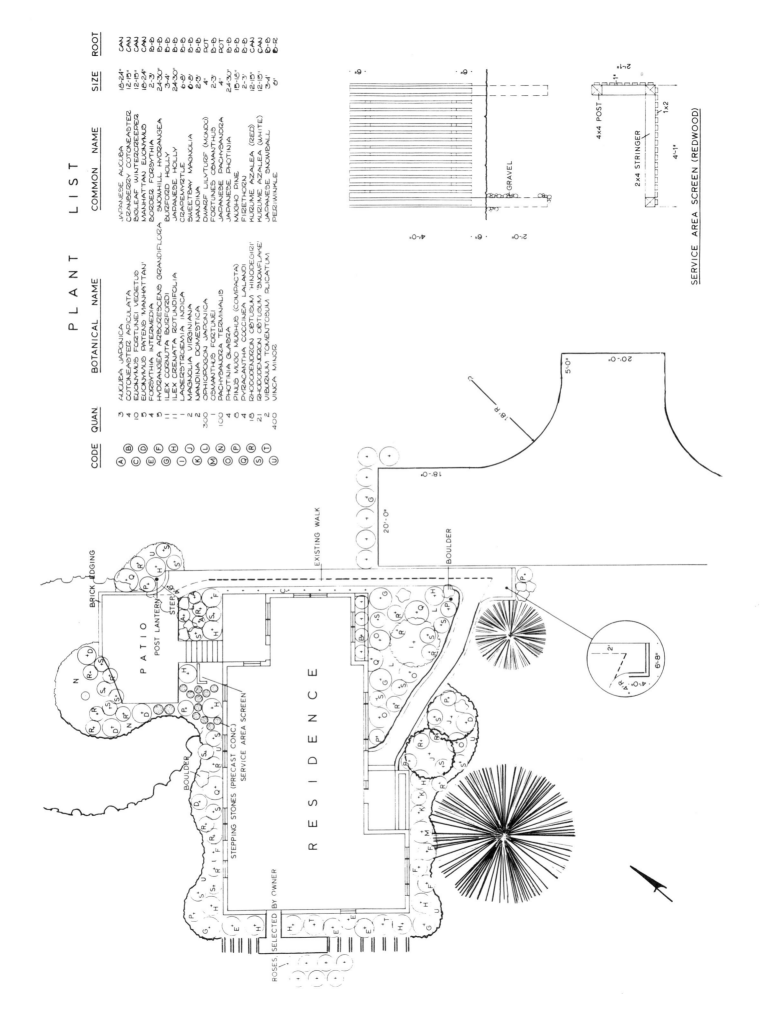

PLANT LIST

CODE	QUAN	BOTANICAL NAME	COMMON NAME	SIZE	ROOT
A	3	AUCUBA JAPONICA	JAPANESE AUCUBA	18-24"	CAN
B	4	COTONEASTER APICULATA	CRANBERRY COTONEASTER	12-15"	CAN
C	10	EUONYMUS FORTUNEI VEGETUS	BIGLEAF WINTERCREEPER	12-15"	CAN
D	5	EUONYMUS PATENS 'MANHATTAN'	MANHATTAN EUONYMUS	18-24"	CAN
E	4	FORSYTHIA INTERMEDIA	BORDER FORSYTHIA	2-3'	B-B
F	9	HYDRANGEA ARBORESCENS GRANDIFLORA	SNOWHILL HYDRANGEA	24-30"	B-B
G	11	ILEX CORNUTA BURFORDI	BURFORD HOLLY	3-4'	B-B
H	11	ILEX CRENATA ROTUNDIFOLIA	JAPANESE HOLLY	24-30"	B-B
I	2	LAGERSTROEMIA INDICA	CRAPEMYRTLE	6-8'	POT
J		MAGNOLIA VIRGINIANA	SWEETBAY MAGNOLIA	6-8'	POT
K	300	OPHIOPOGON JAPONICA	DWARF LILYTURF (MONDO)	4"	POT
L	100	OSMANTHUS FORTUNEI	FORTUNES OSMANTHUS	2-3'	B-B
M	1	PACHYSANDRA TERMINALIS	JAPANESE PACHYSANDRA	4"	POT
N	4	PHOTINIA GLABRA	JAPANESE PHOTINIA	24-30"	B-B
O	6	PINUS MUGO MUGHUS (COMPACTA)	MUGHO PINE	15-18"	B-B
P	9	PYRACANTHA COCCINEA LALANDI	FIRETHORN	2-3'	B-B
Q	18	RHODODENDRON OBTUSUM 'HINODEGIRI'	KURUME AZALEA (RED)	12-15"	CAN
R	21	RHODODENDRON OBTUSUM 'SNOWFLAKE'	KURUME AZALEA (WHITE)	12-15"	CAN
S		VIBURNUM TOMENTOSUM PLICATUM	JAPANESE SNOWBALL	3-4'	B-B
U	400	VINCA MINOR	PERIWINKLE	6"	B-R

SERVICE AREA SCREEN (REDWOOD)

GRAVEL

4×4 POST
2×4 STRINGER
1×2

BRICK EDGING

PATIO

POST LANTERN

STEPPING STONES (PRECAST CONC.)

SERVICE AREA SCREEN

ROSES, SELECTED BY OWNER

RESIDENCE

BOULDER

EXISTING WALK

BOULDER

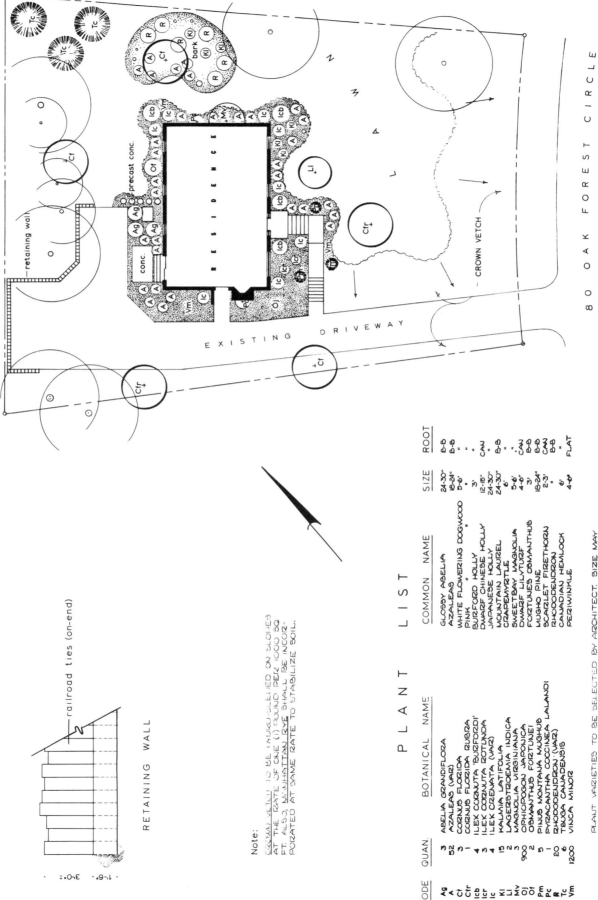

80 OAK FOREST CIRCLE

RESIDENCE

EXISTING DRIVEWAY

retaining wall

precast conc.

conc.

bark

CROWN VETCH

Tc, Tc, Tc

Ct, Ctr, Li

Vm, A, Ic, Icb, Ki, R, O, Ag, Mv, Pc, Oi

---

railroad ties (on-end)

RETAINING WALL

1'-6" · 3'-0" ·

Note:
CROWN VETCH TO BE HYDRO-SEEDED ON SLOPES
AT THE RATE OF ONE (1) POUND PER 1000 SQ
FT. ALSO, MANHATTAN RYE SHALL BE INCOR-
PORATED AT SAME RATE TO STABILIZE SOIL.

P L A N T   L I S T

CODE	QUAN	BOTANICAL NAME	COMMON NAME	SIZE	ROOT
Ag	3	ABELIA GRANDIFLORA	GLOSSY ABELIA	24-30"	B-B
A	52	AZALEAS (VAR)	AZALEAS	18-24"	B-B
Cf	2	CORNUS FLORIDA	WHITE FLOWERING DOGWOOD	5-6'	"
Ctr	1	CORNUS FLORIDA RUBRA	PINK "	"	"
Icb	4	ILEX CORNUTA 'BURFORDI'	BURFORD HOLLY	3'	CAN
Icr	3	ILEX CORNUTA ROTUNDA	DWARF CHINESE HOLLY	12-18"	"
Ic	4	ILEX CRENATA (VAR)	JAPANESE HOLLY	24-30"	"
Kl	15	KALMIA LATIFOLIA	MOUNTAIN LAUREL	6'	B-B
Li	1	LAGERSTROEMIA INDICA	CRAPEMYRTLE	6'	"
Mv	3	MAGNOLIA VIRGINIANA	SWEETBAY MAGNOLIA	5-6'	CAN
Oi	900	OPHIOPOGON JAPONICA	DWARF LILYTURF	4-6"	B-B
Oi	2	OSMANTHUS FORTUNEI	FORTUNES OSMANTHUS	3'	"
Pm	5	PINUS MONTANA MUGHUS	MUGHO PINE	18-24"	B-B
Pc	20	PYRACANTHA COCCINEA LALANDI	SCARLET FIRETHORN	2-3'	CAN
R	6	RHODODENDRON (VAR)	RHODODENDRON	6'	"
Tc		TSUGA CANADENSIS	CANADIAN HEMLOCK		B-B
Vm	1200	VINCA MINOR	PERIWINKLE	4-6"	FLAT

PLANT VARIETIES TO BE SELECTED BY ARCHITECT. SIZE MAY
VARY ACCORDING TO AVAILABILITY. PEAT AND FERTILIZER
SHALL BE INCORPORATED IN ALL PLANTING POCKETS.

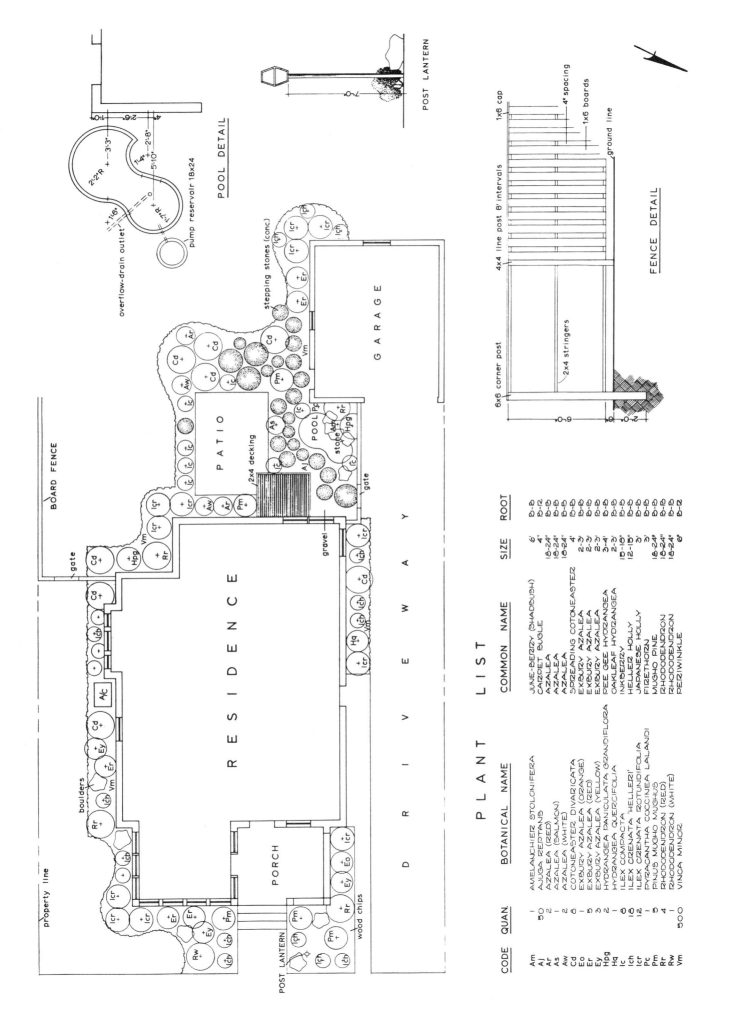

PLANT LIST

CODE	QUAN.	BOTANICAL NAME	COMMON NAME	SIZE	ROOT
Am	1	AMELANCHIER STOLONIFERA	JUNE-BERRY (SHADBUSH)	6'	B-B
Aj	50	AJUGA REPTANS	CARPET BUGLE	4"	P-B
Ar	2	AZALEA (RED)	AZALEA	18-24"	B-B
As	1	AZALEA (SALMON)	AZALEA	18-24"	B-B
Aw	2	AZALEA (WHITE)	AZALEA	18-24"	B-B
Cd	8	COTONEASTER DIVARICATA	SPREADING COTONEASTER	4'	B-B
Eo	5	EXBURY AZALEA (ORANGE)	EXBURY AZALEA	2-3'	B-B
Er	5	EXBURY AZALEA (RED)	EXBURY AZALEA	2-3'	B-B
Ey	3	EXBURY AZALEA (YELLOW)	EXBURY AZALEA	2-3'	B-B
Hpg	2	HYDRANGEA PANICULATA GRANDIFLORA	PEE GEE HYDRANGEA	3-4'	B-B
Hq	1	HYDRANGEA QUERCIFOLIA	OAKLEAF HYDRANGEA	2-3'	B-B
Ic	6	ILEX COMPACTA	INKBERRY	15-18"	B-B
Ich	18	ILEX CRENATA HELLERI'	HELLER HOLLY	12-15"	B-B
Icr	12	ILEX CRENATA ROTUNDIFOLIA	JAPANESE HOLLY	3'	B-B
Pc	5	PYRACANTHA COCCINEA LALANDI	FIRETHORN	18-24"	B-B
Pm	5	PINUS MUGHO MUGHUS	MUGHO PINE	18-24"	B-B
Rr	4	RHODODENDRON (RED)	RHODODENDRON	18-24"	B-B
Rw		RHODODENDRON (WHITE)	RHODODENDRON	6'	B-B
Vm	500	VINCA MINOR	PERIWINKLE		P-B

POOL DETAIL

2'-6"
4'-0"
2'-8"
2'-2" R — 3'-3"
1'-4"
5'-10"
1'-6"
1'-7" R
overflow-drain outlet
pump reservoir 18x24

POST LANTERN

7'-0"

FENCE DETAIL

1x6 cap
4" spacing
1x6 boards
4x4 line post 8' intervals
ground line
6x6 corner post
2x4 stringers
6'-0"
2'-0"

BOARD FENCE
property line
gate
PATIO
2x4 decking
stepping stones (conc.)
GARAGE
POOL
stone
gate
gravel
RESIDENCE
boulders
PORCH
POST LANTERN
wood chips
DRIVEWAY

PLANT LIST

CODE	QUAN.	BOTANICAL NAME	COMMON NAME	SIZE	ROOT
A	2	ACER PALMATUM ATROPURPUREUM	JAPANESE RED MAPLE	6'	CAN
B	1	ACER PLATANOIDES 'CRIMSON KING'	CRIMSON KING MAPLE	8-10'	B-B
C	21	AZALEA (VAR)	AZALEA	18-24"	CAN
D	2	BETULA PAPYRIFERA	PAPER BIRCH	8-10'	B-B
E	2	BUXUS SEMPERVIRENS	AMERICAN BOXWOOD	18-24"	B-B
F	1	CORNUS FLORIDA	WHITE FLOWERING DOGWOOD	6'	B-B
G	1	CORNUS FLORIDA RUBRA	PINK DOGWOOD	6'	B-B
H	8	EUONYMUS ALATUS	WINGED EUONYMUS	2'	B-B
I	5	EUONYMUS PATENS 'MANHATTAN'	MANHATTAN EUONYMUS	24-30"	B-B
J	2	ILEX AQUIFOLIUM	ENGLISH HOLLY	24-30"	CAN
K	12	ILEX CORNUTA 'NELLIE STEVENS'	NELLIE R. STEVENS HOLLY	2-3'	CAN
L	8	ILEX CORNUTA ROTUNDA	DWARF CHINESE HOLLY	15-18"	CAN
M	8	ILEX CRENATA ROTUNDIFOLIA	ROUNDLEAF JAPANESE HOLLY	24-30"	CAN
N	4	KALMIA LATIFOLIA	MOUNTAIN LAUREL	3'	B-B
O	5	LAGERSTROEMIA INDICA	CRAPEMYRTLE	6'	CAN
P	600	LIRIOPE MUSCARI	BIGBLUE LIRIOPE	8-10"	CAN
Q	1	MAGNOLIA GRANDIFLORA	SOUTHERN MAGNOLIA	6-8'	B-B
R	250	OPHIOPOGON JAPONICA	MONDO GRASS	4-6"	POT
S	8	PINUS MUGO MUGHUS	MUGHO PINE	15-18"	CAN
T	4	PINUS STROBUS	EASTERN WHITE PINE	10-12'	B-B
U	1	PYRACANTHA COCCINEA LALANDI	FIRETHORN	2-3'	CAN
V	1	QUERCUS PALUSTRIS	PIN OAK	8-10'	B-B
W	2	QUERCUS PHELLOS	WILLOW OAK	8-10'	B-B
X	11	RHODODENDRON (VAR)	RHODODENDRON	3'	B-B
Y	6	TSUGA CANADENSIS	CANADIAN HEMLOCK	6-8'	B-B
Z	1200	VINCA MINOR	PERIWINKLE	4-6"	POT

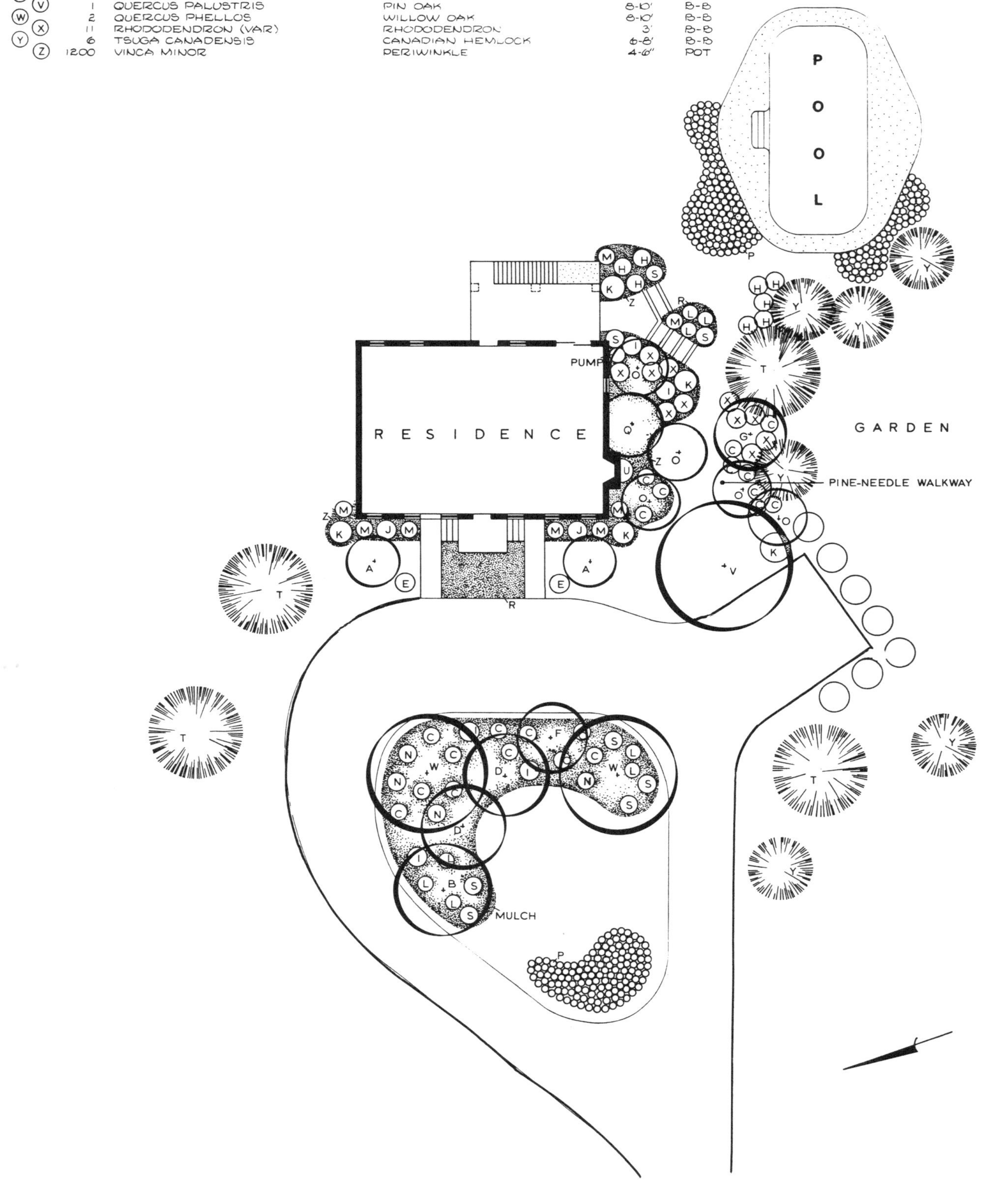

POOL
RESIDENCE
PUMP
GARDEN
PINE-NEEDLE WALKWAY
MULCH

   Frequently a cluster of native trees may appear in the lawn area, having been preserved during the site development operations. Dense shade and extensive root systems obviously are not conducive to the growing of grass. Vegetative colonies may be contained within an "island" of mulch and/or ground cover, thereby creating visual interest while eliminating a difficult lawn maintenance situation (Fig. 6.29). Additional trees and azalea-type shrubs may strengthen the aesthetic character of the insular compositions (Figs. 6.30 and 6.31).
   The development of residential properties should reflect the attitudes and preferences of the owners, accommodating their particular style of habitation. Contemporary modes of living often preclude the allocation of evenings and weekends for the care of home grounds. Today's culture demands low maintenance landscaping innovations. The designer's approach therefore must be practical, straightforward, and yet imaginative. The foregoing planning techniques address themselves to fundamental considerations.

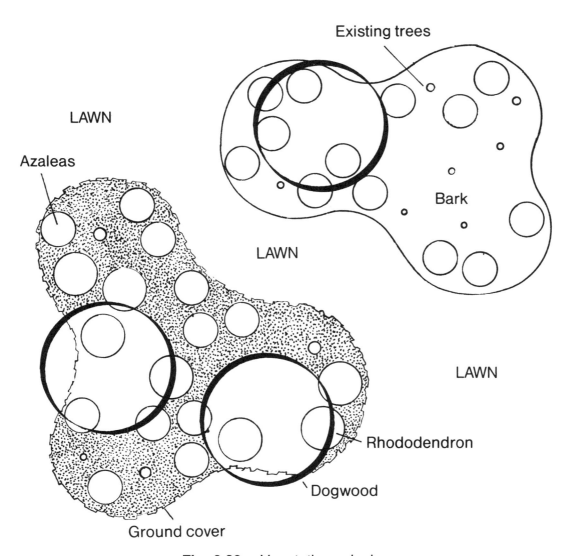

Fig. 6.29.   Vegetative colonies

Fig. 6.30. Colonized trees

Fig. 6.31. Mulch "island"

7

Elements and Principles of Visual Composition

Ever has it been that man seeks inner peace, a state of being devoid of conflict, free of tension. A restful mood is induced by harmonious art forms, whether expressed by the composite of musical notes, the metaphor of language, the shapes and textures of sculptured clay or chiseled stone, the spectrum of assorted pigments, or perhaps the human figure in motion. Art may be defined as the orderly selection and arrangement or design of an elemental substance, either real or abstract, measured in time and/or space. In music, the choice of note pitch and duration, in literature, the choice of words, and in visual art, the choice of lines, textures, colors—all serve to produce an artistic composition, the success of which is governed by its effect on the human spirit.

The fine arts of design generally refer to painting, drawing, architecture, and sculpture, as opposed to the performing arts. Visual art is depicted by two-dimensional abstractions and three-dimensional objects, graphics often suggesting the third dimension through mental perception. Architecture merely transforms two-dimensional concepts to third-dimensional realities. Essentially, in discussing the elements and principles of design, whether one is preoccupied with the two-dimensional abstractions of the artist or the third-dimensional shapes and textures of construction materials and living plants is of little consequence, excepting the fact that plant configurations are affected by time.

Elements of Design

The elements of visual design are *line*, *direction*, *shape*, *size*, *texture*, *value*, and *color*. A line is either straight or curved. The direction of a line may be horizontal, vertical, or oblique. Connecting lines determine shapes, ranging from angular to curvilinear. Size refers to the length and width of the line, the area of the shape, and/or the interval or distance between lines and shapes. Texture may range from coarse to smooth and is indicative of the structural characteristics of lines and shapes. Value refers to the extremes of white and black and intermediate shades of gray. Color or hue is derived from the admixture of the primary pigments, red, yellow, and blue, in varying proportions.

It should become apparent that each of the elements can manifest itself in an extremely contrasting fashion. For example, a line may be straight as opposed to semicircular. Two straight lines may be perpendicular, showing directional contrast, or parallel, showing harmony. Diametrically opposed shapes are represented by the circle and the triangle; the perimeter of a circle is a smooth, continuous, connecting curve, while that of the triangle involves abrupt angles.

The elements, then, manifest themselves in varying degrees of similarity or dissimilarity (Fig. 7.1). Illustratively, two shapes may be represented as identical circles, one may be larger than the other (size contrast), or the two shapes may be depicted as dissimilar configurations altogether (one being curvilinear; the other, angular). According to Maitland Graves (1951), all art structures are based on three fundamental qualities: *repetition* (identical elements), *harmony* (similar elements), and *discord* (totally different elements).

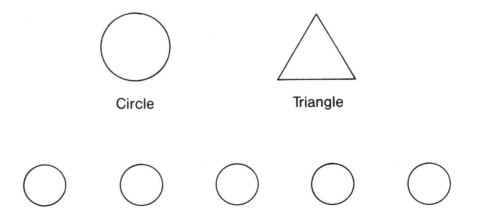

Circle   Triangle

Fig. 7.1. Similarity versus dissimilarity. (*Top*) extreme contrast; (*bottom*) monotonous repetition.

The compositional grouping of design elements should create interest through the variation of shape, size, color, etc., devoid of overbearingly harsh contrast. On the other hand, a continuum of identical elements lends itself to monotonous repetition. It must be remembered that a restful psychological response is induced by stimuli evoking interest and suggesting harmony. So, we may conclude that discord and monotonous repetition generally are extremes to be avoided in selecting and arranging adjacent design elements. Quite simply, moderate elemental variations are conducive to harmonious relationships. Tranquility is suggested by somewhat subtle elemental alterations. Of course, a bold, dramatic effect is achieved by introducing sudden contrast. These concepts are illustrated in Figs. 7.2 and 7.3.

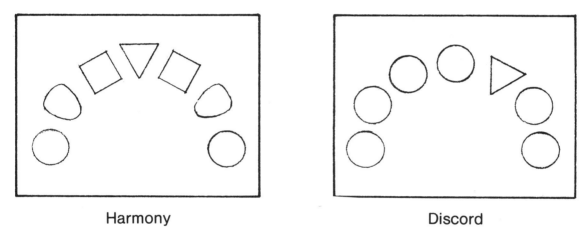

Harmony   Discord

Fig. 7.2.   Shape contrast. (*Left*) Gradual transition from curvilinear to angular; (*right*) Sudden contrast.

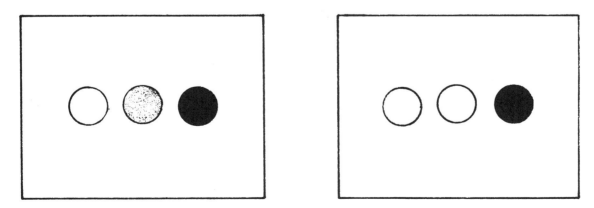

Fig. 7.3.   Tonal contrast. (*Left*) Intermediate gray softens transition; (*right*) Transition too abrupt.

Thus, although compositions may contain *diametrically opposed elements* (a circle and a triangle, for instance), such elements normally *should not occur side by side*; other less contrasting elemental variations (in this case, ovals and squares) should separate the extremes so that the changes between adjacent elements are gradual. Likewise, the extremes of white and black should be separated by intermediate tones of gray in order to "soften" the transition.

Visual compositions of artistic merit, then, evolve from the disciplined process of choosing and juxtaposing design elements of varying but nonetheless psychologically compatible characteristics, much like the selecting of harmonious sounds in music. This is not to say that one must avoid arousing man's primitive instincts through the *occasional* use of discordant elemental combinations, nor that to do so necessarily would be in bad taste. Nature, however, generally is not offensive in coordinating seasonal color and surface textures, so it would seem that the landscape designer should follow her pattern.

An understanding of elemental relationships is essential when selecting and positioning plants. For example, pyramidal forms do not harmonize with the somewhat circular (globular) shapes of many shrubs (Fig. 7.4). The size contrast of adjacent shrubs should be carefully considered (as well as leaf texture and flower color) (Fig. 7.5).

Theoretically, discord connotes maximum elemental variance between (adjacent) objects. Harmony exists when one or more factors are similar. Complete harmony is synonymous with repetition; all elemental aspects of the objects being compared are identical. Plants may appear discordant in shape or size relationships, while manifesting harmony in other dimensions (e.g., similarity of texture, color). Most trees and shrubs exhibit at least one common characteristic; therefore, discord in the landscape seldom is absolute.

Texture is determined by the size and arrangement of the constituent parts of any substance. Coarse surfaces generally exhibit strong tonal contrasts, whereas finely textured, smooth surfaces appear somewhat glossy. Coarse-textured (plant) materials are visually more prominent than fine-textured varieties, often employed to accent points in the landscape. On the other hand, fine-textured shrubs characteristically recede (appear more distant). Therefore, an illusion of greater depth may be created by placing coarse-textured materials in the foreground of compositions, to be flanked or backed by finer textures.

Fig. 7.4.   Extreme shape contrast in the landscape.

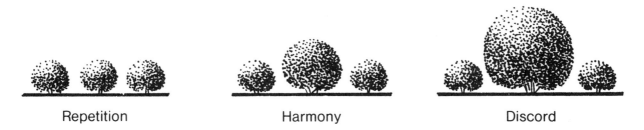

Repetition   Harmony   Discord

Fig. 7.5.   Plant size comparisons. (*Left*) Total similarity; (*middle*) pleasant
contrast; (*right*) contrast too great.

Fig. 7.6. Prominent coarse texture

Fig. 7.7. Transitional grouping

In Fig. 7.6, the darker tones dominate, strongly defining the form of the central plant. Often visually heavy, coarse materials are fronted with smaller "facer" plants of medium-to-fine textures, thereby providing a transition between the dominant plant and the softer textures of the ground plane and/or other shrubs. In Fig. 7.7 the smaller plants also serve to conceal the lower stem structure of larger specimens.

Value denotes tonal quality, a visual effect produced by varying intensities of illumination, coupled with the amount of light absorbed and/or reflected by a particular substance. Pure black manifests total absorption; white, total reflection. Texture obviously influences the distribution of light on a given surface, depending on the angle of the illuminating rays. Highlights and shades indicate differing levels of exposure. The larger the constituent surface particles of any material, the more pronounced the shaded areas become, when the light source is less than 90° overhead. Tonal contrasts, then, generally are proportionate to the size of the surface irregularities, other factors being equal. That is why coarse textures manifest darker values.

White, of course, is not a true color. When placed in the foreground of planting arrangements, its tonal quality inherently tends to increase the apparent depth of the composition, much like coarse-textured materials. Conversely, when positioned in the background, white values "advance," thus minimizing the illusion of distance. Snow-capped mountains seem less distant. The vividness of white sand traps clearly defines golf course greens, thereby improving the golfer's depth perception.

Bright colors enhance visual effects, but must be used with discretion when selecting plant materials. The seasonal flush of chromatic dominance should not become an end in itself; other elemental considerations are equally important. Generally, a particular hue should be represented by the grouping of identical plants, as opposed to the selection of single specimens of varying colorations. That is to say, the spotty effect of a multitude of colors should be avoided; a limited variety of colors well represented is preferable. Pastels blend favorably with most garden styles, accentuated by stronger chromatic values where attention is to be focused.

Perhaps the most disturbing color combination is exhibited by various shades of red displayed against (red) brick walls. If this cannot be eliminated altogether, incompatible tones should be separated by the introduction of white blossoms and/or rich evergreen foliage.

Principles of Design

Art form structuring is guided by established principles expressive of the manner in which various design elements are disposed within a given space, be it the artist's canvas or the confines of a garden courtyard. The principles of design are *unity*, *balance*, *rhythm*, *harmony*, and *dominance* (center of interest).

Unity

Unity refers to the interdependence of constituent parts to form a whole; each component or element therefore contributes to the total being of something, whether abstract or real. Organization and singleness of purpose characterize unity, without which artistic endeavors appear fragmented, lacking clarity of expression. In its simplest form, unity is expressed by the repetition of identical elements. A series of portholes on an ocean liner, geese in flight, a row of cornstalks in a field, or even the uniforms of marching band members visually reflect basic unity. Although the repetition of identical elements lends itself to monotony if not given relief through elemental variations, identical elements should be repeated often enough to establish consistency in the composition.

Plants in the landscape should be limited in kind and variety in order to produce a unified effect. Too many divergent shapes, textures, colors, etc., generate confusion. Essentially, the prevalence of one, two, or three species serves to identify style and establish consistency, while other somewhat subservient plant materials in garden compositions simply fill space, add interest, and perhaps afford seasonal change.

Balance

Balance influences eye movement. Lines and shapes have visual "weight," or visual magnetism. As shown in Fig. 7.8, a heavy line attracts the eye more than a thin line of equal length. To create a psychological sense of balance, the thin line would have to be extended to a point at which its total mass, or visual weight, equalled that of the heavier line.

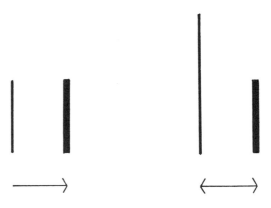

Fig. 7.8. Eye movement

Formal, or symmetrical, balance is achieved when identical elements are positioned equidistantly from a central axis, or line of vision. An algebraic analogy may be expressed in the formula: $a + b = a + b$. The factors a and b are identical (on either side of the equation), and one side of the equation balances, or equals, the other (Fig. 7.9 left).

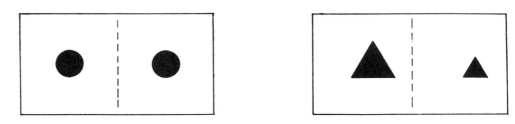

Fig. 7.9. Formal (*left*) versus informal (optical) balance (*right*)

Informal, or optical, balance is achieved when the visual weight of dissimilar elements (objects) irregularly positioned to either side of a central axis is equal; i.e., eye movement to either side of a central axis is equal, even though the elements attracting the eye are dissimilar. An algebraic analogy in this case might be: $m + n = o + p$; the factors are dissimilar, yet the equation balances (Fig. 7.9 right).

Graphically, the axial line of vision should lie within the middle portion of a drawing or composition. The elements should appear balanced within the confines of the composition so that the eye, glancing from one element or group of elements to another, comes to rest, so to speak, in the central area of the composition. This is not to say that the dominant, or primary, feature must be positioned in the middle of the arrangement. Eye movement itself, however, though being influenced by the possibly off-centered dominant feature, will focus again on the central portion of the composition as a result of the counter-attraction of secondary features positioned to the side opposite that of the dominant feature. This concept is illustrated in Fig. 7.10

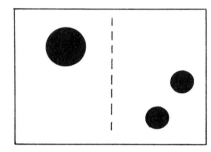

Fig. 7.10.   "Balanced" Composition

Formal buildings normally require a formal balancing of plant materials flanking the corners and to either side of the central entrance (axial line of vision). As illustrated in Fig. 7.11 (left), the larger plants are situated at the corners, followed by those at the entrance. Again, the corresponding plants on either side of the central entrance are identical in size, variety, and spacing.

The imaginary axis of asymmetrical architecture likewise should lie in the center of the elevational view, though doors and windows may appear irregularly. The corner plants illustrated in Fig. 7.11 (right) represent relatively large evergreens, followed in size by the plants to the right of the entrance and between the windows, respectively. The remaining plants could be smaller sized deciduous specimens (see Chapter 6).

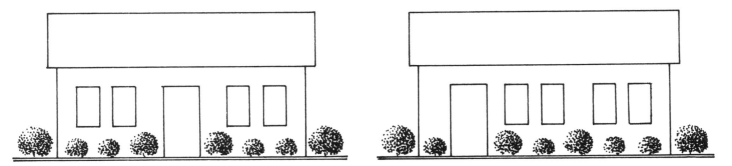

Fig. 7.11.   Formal (*left*) versus informal (*right*) planting balance

Rhythm

Rhythm expresses the degree of animation within a composition. Does it seem alive, or flat and dull; is it free and fluid, sequential; is there a regular recurrence of like features? Rhythm may be thought of as measured repetition; the measured interval of elements influences the progressive rapidity, or crescendo, of eye movement. Rhythm can be exemplified by the ripples generated when a stone is cast into a pool of water; the concentric circles enlarge in a cadenced, or measured, form of repetition.

The changes of the seasons alone creates rhythm. Deciduous vegetative forms obviously provide optimum interest with the approach of fall and spring, culminated by the anticipation of flowering buds. The somewhat static quality of coniferous evergreens can be enlivened with contrasts in size and variety. The orderly spacing of secondary plants, coupled with the recurring emphasis of a dominant specimen, suggests rhythm, analogous to the time interval or frequency of musical notes accentuated by a dominant beat. The grouping of certain species to create mass is similar to the orchestration of chords. The motif of a building facade manifests a recurrence of constant dimensions (modular door and window openings, perhaps); hence, rhythm. "*Architecture* is . . . frozen music" (Schelling).

Harmony

Harmony and unity are often thought of as interchangeable terms. Harmony should not be restricted, however, to the generalized connotation of unity or consistency, referring more to the creative *variances* of design elements that are intended to heighten interest without becoming discordant. And, unity may refer simply to the spatial relationships of compositional parts.

Dominance

Dominance connotes emphasis and strength, or the preponderance of certain elemental forces. Without visual centers of interest, compositions appear disoriented, and unity is weakened. Dominance gives direction, attracting the eye to a climactic focal point.

Not all elements of design necessarily manifest themselves in all compositions. For example, an abstract line drawing may be devoid of halftones and color; the foliage of plants often obscures the structural lines of stems and branches. The elements merely serve as basic compositional ingredients to be chosen with discretion. However, all artistic arrangements should be criticized objectively with an awareness of the five principles of design.

"Scale" and "proportion" are qualities of art reflecting size relationships. In landscape architecture, the human figure is generally regarded as the standard of size comparison; thus, the "human" scale. The height of man influences the dimensions of environmental design elements. Obviously, objects at or near eye level are observed with greater scrutiny than those well above or below a particular visual plane. "Perspective," of course, affects the concept of size; a mountain range or a city skyscraper is much less imposing at a distance than when viewed from its base. A psychological sense of enclosure is proportionate to the horizontal and/or vertical distance between the observer and the thing observed. Designers must be aware, then, of eye level when creating spatial illusions.

Proportion refers to the relative size of components. The head of a well-proportioned human figure should be one-seventh of the total body height; the width of an entrance walk to a large residence should be no less than 5 ft, depending on personal judgment. Through the years, various concepts of proportion have been "accepted" as standards by which art is evaluated. One such standard is the "Golden Mean," a ratio of 1:1.618. An example of the Golden Mean proportion is the division of a line into two segments of unequal length (Fig. 7.12).

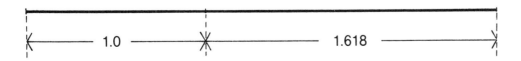

Fig. 7.12.   Golden Mean proportion

The dimensions of a rectangle may assume the proportions of 1:1:618, constructed whereby radius B is extended from the midpoint of one side of a square, and deflected as shown to form the longer side of the rectangle (Fig. 7.13).

The design significance of the Golden Mean lies in its appeal to the human senses, though often one cannot explain why certain proportions are more pleasing than others (subliminal effect). Furthermore, there seldom is unanimity of opinion regarding the quality of art. Nonetheless, basic design principles, along with various concepts of scale and proportion, have withstood the test of time, and should be recognized as a matter of historical precedence.

The numbers 8, 13, 21, 34, 55, etc., represent a progression of Golden Mean multiples; i.e., $1.618 \times 8 =$ (approx.) 13, $1.618 \times 13 = 21$, or, stated another way, $8/13 = 13/21 = 1/1.618$. The ratio of $55/89$ is the closest whole number equivalent to 1:1.618. In a practical application, the numbers 5, 8, 13, 21, etc., could represent dimensions in a landscape design. For instance, the Golden Mean rectangle may be assigned the measurements of 5 ft $\times$ 8 ft, or 8 ft $\times$ 13 ft, appropriate dimensions, say, for an entrance landing or patio. Of course, any combination of numbers, or dimensions, can be derived from the Golden Mean proportion.

Fig. 7.13. Golden Mean rectangle

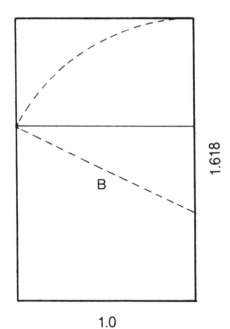

1.0

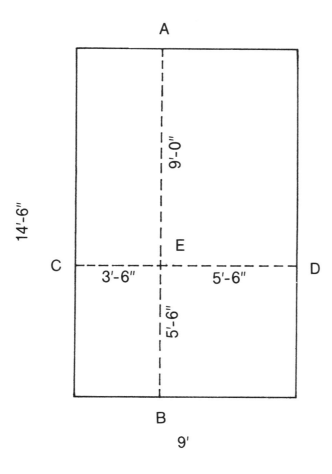

Fig. 7.14. Patio dimensioning

To illustrate the application of the 1:1.618 proportion, assume a level surface measuring 9 ft × 14 ft − 6 in., conveniently approximating a Golden Mean rectangle. Furthermore, suppose a patio of those dimensions is to be constructed of concrete, perhaps washed for a textural effect. Added visual interest can be achieved by first subdividing the rectangular space as shown in Fig. 7.14, where essentially, $CD:AB = CE:ED = BE:EA = 1:1.618$.

In Fig. 7.15A, 2 in. × 4 in. redwood dividers are centered on-edge along the *AB-CD* lines. The conceptual simplicity of the surface treatment affords an interesting pattern that may be repeated *ad infinitum*; i.e., various dimensions can be further subdivided in accordance with the Golden Mean. It must be remembered, however, that larger spaces like courtyards and plazas, for example, lend themselves to a greater variety of lines, shapes, textures, etc. Smaller areas too often are over-designed.

Figure 7.15B shows a band of brick headers along the *AB* line. Of course, both patio illustrations could be edged with headers or rowlocks (bricks on edge) for yet another visual effect.

Generally, the first priority in the designing of space for human use and enjoyment is that of function. The landscape architect is retained primarily to resolve specific utilitarian aspects of a planned environment. However, while accommodating various program objectives, one must be ever mindful of the visual quality of the end results; an awareness of the elements and principles of composition thus becomes essential. The ultimate aesthetic value of any landscaping and planning endeavor should be appreciated as well as functional economy.

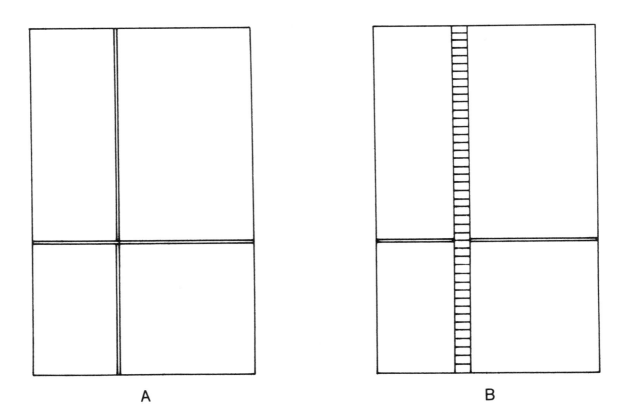

A   B

Fig. 7.15. Surface patterns

Fig. 7.16.   City Hall Plaza, Memphis, Tennessee

8

The Art of Garden Design

The elements of design—line, direction, shape, size, texture, value, and color—and the principles of composition—unity, balance, rhythm, harmony, and dominance— serve as guidelines for the creation of art. The graphic illustrator employs pen and pencil, coupled with an array of pigments, to compose his particular fantasy. The interior designer coordinates furniture and fabrics. Earth mounds, water, trees and shrubs, ground cover, and basic construction materials, such as wood, brick, stone, and concrete, represent the real elements available to the landscape architect in creating various environmental effects. Quite simply, the selection and arrangement of two-dimensional abstractions and the grouping of third-dimensional objects, respectively, are governed theoretically by identical artistic sensitivities. Whatever the medium, all forms of art evolve from an understanding of and an appreciation for *order.* To illustrate the basic approach to garden design, the formal, or symmetrical, concept of composition versus the informal, or asymmetrical, will be discussed (see Figs. 8.1 and 8.2).

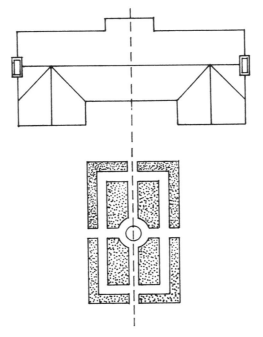
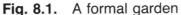

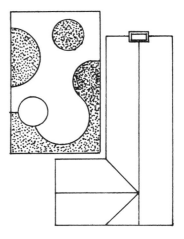

Fig. 8.1. A formal garden   **Fig. 8.2.** An informal terrace

A Formal Garden

A formal garden reflects tradition, and is associated with formal architecture; the style of architecture should influence the landscape design philosophy. The casualness of informality is associated with contemporary (modern) styles of architecture, though the disciplines of order nonetheless serve their function; optical, or informal, balance perhaps is more difficult to achieve than formal balance. The development of a tract of land measuring 38 ft × 60 ft (conveniently approximating the Golden Mean proportion!) shall serve to exemplify contrasting methods of design; i.e., formal versus informal.

A formal design concept requires the establishment of both a major and minor axis. These are the central lines of vision. This is accomplished by dividing each dimension of the proposed rectangular garden (as shown in Fig. 8.3), and connecting the midpoints A, B and C, D, respectively, with imaginary axial lines. The crossing of the lines determines the center of the composition. Walks are located on the axial lines, leading to a (proposed) dominant central feature, or focal point. The preliminary plan serves to organize space. The two-dimensional line and shape relationships defining use areas must be artistically conceived, in accordance with the principles of composition and an awareness of both human and plant space requirements.

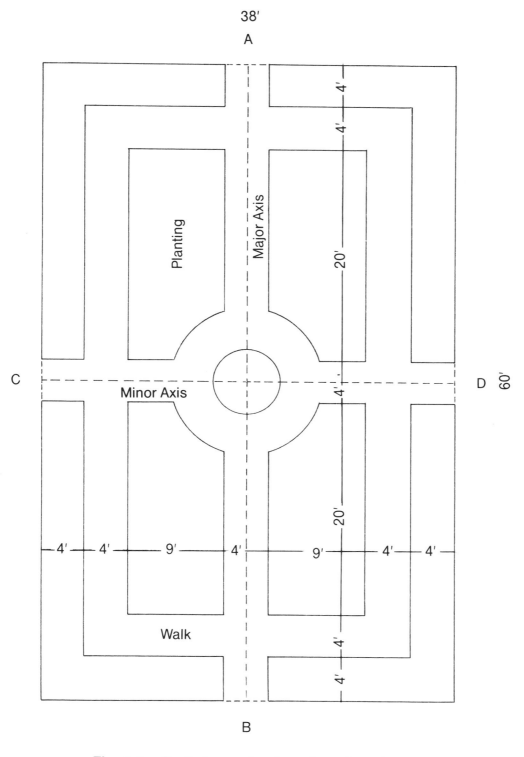

Fig. 8.3. Preliminary plan for a formal garden

The final plan (representing the third dimension) must appeal to the senses as a work of art in itself, reflecting balance and proportion (Fig. 8.4). If the two-dimensional plan or drawing is not aesthetically pleasing, chances are the completed garden likewise will fall short of its potential. Do not rely on the eventual color of flowering plants or the camouflaging effect of foliage to conceal a design weakness in the graphic illustration. Furthermore, specific third-dimensional construction and/or plant materials are not of particular importance during the preliminary stages of planning until the desired effect within each use area has been coordinated (hard surface versus soft, low planting versus high, evergreen versus deciduous, etc.). Once the elemental design relationships of the various areas and the objects therein have been determined, then third-dimensional materials are selected to fulfill the design requirements.

To emphasize the significance of the central feature in the formal garden as a focal point (here represented by a statue, thereby stressing verticality), the adjacent planting beds should contain low-growth materials such as grass or other forms of ground cover (depicted by the stippled texture). The interior panels might be further defined with edging material (smaller circles) reaching a height of, say, 18 in. The peripheral planting beds should be strengthened visually with medium-to-large evergreens, positioned in the corners and on either side of the access points (thus defining the over-all dimensions of the garden). Additional plantings, serving as filler material (represented by the staggered circles) between the proposed evergreens, may introduce color and perhaps seasonal variations in foliage, if in fact they are deciduous in nature. The stippled effect in the outer beds should not represent grass, but rather other forms of maintenance-free ground cover and/or mulching material such as wood chips, cotton boll hulls (in the South), or darkened Michigan peat.

An analysis of the formal garden plan in Fig. 8.4 reveals that the five principles of composition have been recognized. Unity is manifested by the repetition of circular shapes. The size contrast of the circles, representing different plants, affords interest through variety. The circular walk in the center of the garden composition (coupled with the adjacent semicircular planting arrangements) breaks the monotony of the otherwise straight-line space configurations. Formal balance is achieved quite obviously by the identicality of the four quadrants of the composition, having been guided by the establishment of a major and a minor axis (center lines). The staggered arrangement of the filler plants along the outer margins creates a sense of movement, or rhythm. The mood of the composition is one of restraint; the elemental contrasts are moderate, thus producing a restful, harmonious effect. The centrally located statue dominates the garden scene, giving direction to both eye movement and pedestrian circulation, in that one's natural impulse is to amble toward the point of visual attraction.

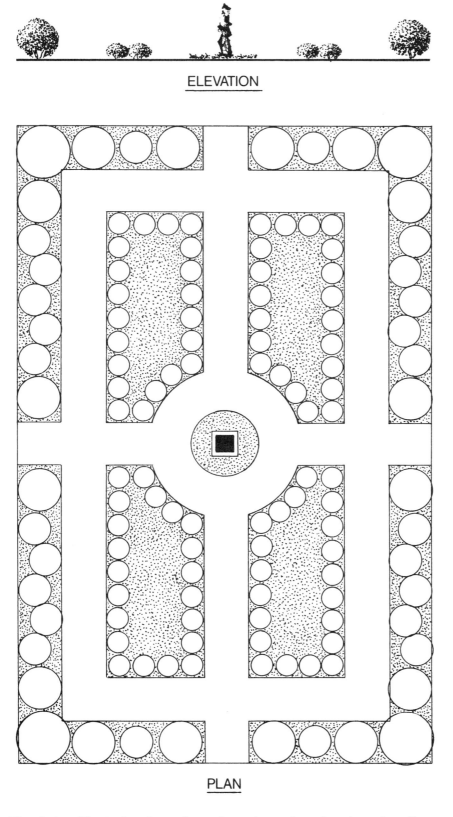

ELEVATION

PLAN

Fig. 8.4. Final plan for a formal garden, also showing elevation

An informal design concept, either rectilinear or curvilinear, on the other hand, requires the establishment of space relationships (balance and proportion) that can be measured without the convenience of a central line of vision from which objects, or elements, are positioned in an equidistant fashion. While the center of a doorway or window may serve to establish the mid-axis or reference line of a formal garden, the objects of an informal grouping relate more unto themselves; an imaginary center line may serve to determine over-all balance, but is not required to establish uniformity; there is none. The irregular occurrence of elements in an informal garden, such as planting beds, walks, fountains, is analogous to the arrangement of notes in syncopated music. Intuition, or feeling, for optical balance rarely can be relied on without first having understood the disciplines of informal order. Free-form, fanciful arrangements may appear to reflect an uninhibited, care-free approach to design, but nonetheless, great art is often judged according to mathematical analytics. The universe itself manifests the science of measured distance, correlating with size, or space intervals, as an element of design.

An Abstract Garden Courtyard

The Golden Mean rectangle at our disposal lends itself to further mathematical exploitation. Each dimension can be divided (as shown in Fig. 8.5) so that the resultant line segments are proportioned approximately in the ratio, 1:1.6 (*AE:EB* = 23 ft : 37 ft; *CE:ED* = 14.5 ft : 23.5 ft). By connecting corresponding points thus established on parallel dimensions (*A* to *B* and *C* to *D*, for example), the rectangle can be subdivided *ad infinitum*.

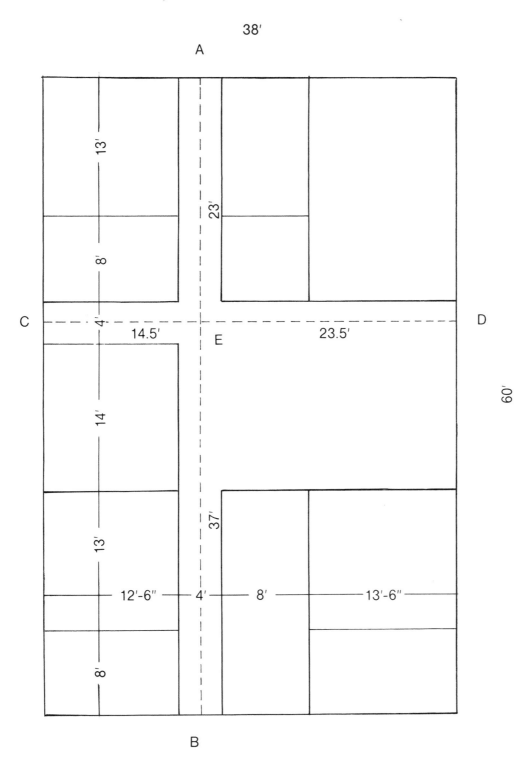

Fig. 8.5. Preliminary plan for an informal garden courtyard

In the preliminary plan for an informal courtyard, a 4 ft walk has been centered on the *AB*, *CD* axial lines. The remaining areas have been subdivided as done previously; e.g., 8 ft : 13 ft approximates the Golden Mean. Each area thus created may not (and probably will not) result consistently in the intended (Golden Mean) proportion; some spaces may become squares, or nearly so. However, this technique establishes sufficient control to produce a pleasing composition. The designer must use discretion in the arrangement of various shapes to maintain a sense of optical balance. Once the shapes have been determined and the pedestrian areas established, various landscape materials are considered for the desired effect within the garden. The smaller random-sized circles shown in the final plan for an abstract or informal courtyard (Fig. 8.6) represent river stone. The larger circles represent low-growth plant material such as Heller holly (*Ilex crenata* 'helleri') or perhaps dwarf ('gumpo') azaleas. The stippled texture represents some form of ground cover, depending on the degree of exposure to the sun. One of the three pool areas is accentuated by a fountain, thus serving as the focal point. Each mass of materials is defined and/or separated by either the proposed pedestrian way or 2 in. × 4 in. redwood dividers, on edge.

The concept of two-dimensional abstractions is superbly manifested by the works of the Dutch painter, Pieter Mondriaan (1872–1944). Originally a landscape artist stressing mass devoid of detail, Mondriaan became obsessed with the straight-line, rectilinear forms of art. The Golden Mean method of establishing outdoor areas produces effects quite similar to the Mondriaan style.

Contrary to the Mondriaan antipathy for curves, an earlier eighteenth century school of thought existed 'abhoring a straight line,' to paraphrase the design philosophy of an English landscape gardener nicknamed "Capability" Brown. They vehemently advocated that curves in the landscape are identified with nature. Straight-line geometric configurations, on the other hand, reflect the imposition of man-made order on the physical world, and often manifest themselves in marked contrast to the undulations and irregularities of naturalistic settings.

Buildings for the most part are rectilinear, thus suggesting straight-line landscape architectural treatments. Tennis courts obviously require angular spaces, as do most parking lots. The customs and functional habits of man seem to demand certain geometric considerations in site planning. The symmetry of a formal garden affords a sense of repose, and is a delight to those who appreciate classic design. The intent here is not to debate the superiority of the straight line versus the curve, but merely to point out the appropriateness of each in the landscape according to feeling and/or function.

A common responsibility of the landscape architect is to "soften" architectural facades with plant materials and to create a visual transition from the traditional angular aspects of buildings to the free-form, curvilinear character of the natural environment. The mathematical relationship of curves is perhaps difficult to establish, except to identify a common radius (repetition). The reverse curve is one of the most pleasing lines to behold, and its use in the landscape may apply to garden seat walls, the outline of planting beds, or even to broad, gracefully sweeping steps in a lawn accommodating grade changes (consisting of only two or three risers). The noted landscape architect Thomas Church artfully employed the reverse curve, as did J. Duke Moody of Memphis, Tennessee.

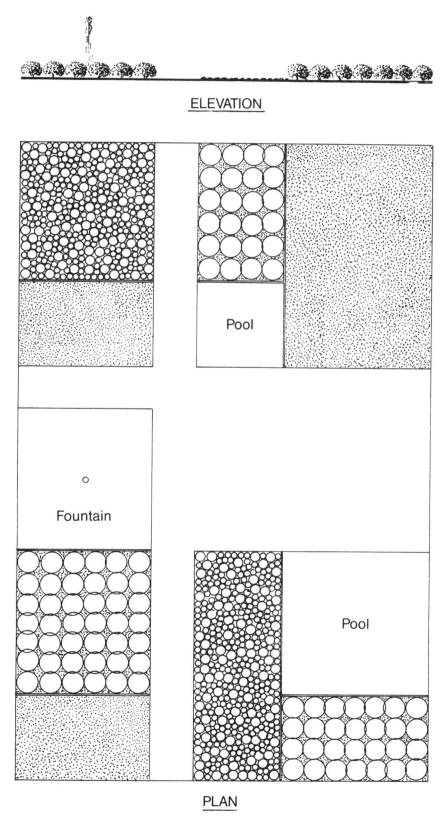

ELEVATION

PLAN

Fig. 8.6. Final plan for an abstract or informal courtyard, also showing elevation.

A Curvilinear Terrace

The preliminary plan shown in Fig. 8.7 for a curvilinear terrace (utilizing the 38 ft × 60 ft tract of land) consists almost exclusively of curved lines. The larger (12 ft) radius of the reverse curve is repeated in the semicircle. The composition appears to be balanced, and the proportions of the circles and curves seem to be compatible. A dominant feature or focal point will be incorporated in the final plan. Obviously, art is not a pure science; adherence to specific "rules" will not guarantee artistic success. And, the arrangement and relationship of various lines and shapes cannot always be subjected to mathematical interpretations. Personal judgment, then, must play an important role in the creation of art forms, without forsaking the principles of composition.

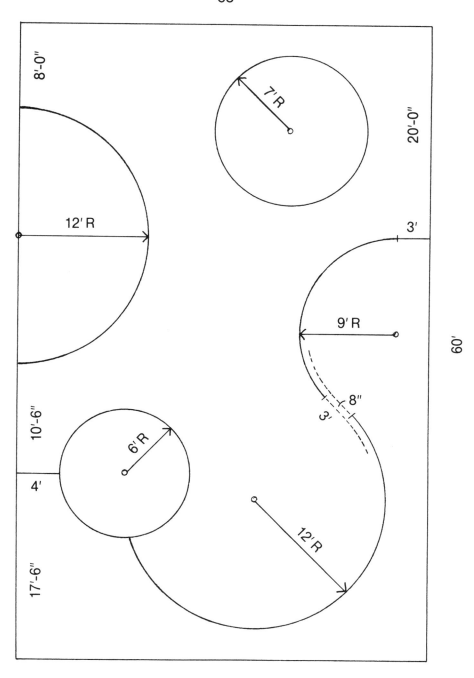

Fig. 8.7. Preliminary plan for a curvilinear terrace

In the final plan for a curvilinear terrace (Fig. 8.8), the various planting areas have been edged with brick, positioned as "headers" (laid flat, with the ends perpendicular to the planting beds, thereby affording a visually strong 8 in. border). The surface area for pedestrian use might consist of washed concrete (exposed aggregate); brick, in various patterns; flagstone, either bluestone or slate; or simply ¼ in. pea gravel. The fountain-pool should be elevated at least 4 in., thus defining its presence, acting as a safety factor, and protecting the water somewhat from surface debris that may accumulate on the terrace. The reverse curve could serve very well as a seat wall, being elevated approximately 18 in. and structured to accommodate a cap measuring no less than 13 in. wide; the perimeter of the pool should be at least as high as the seat wall, perhaps becoming part of it. The various circles (representing shrubs) should indicate a mixture of evergreen and deciduous plant materials, providing both seasonal flowers and year-round greenery. (Trees have been omitted from this and previous garden plans in this chapter so that the reader may concentrate on the base plane of the drawings.)

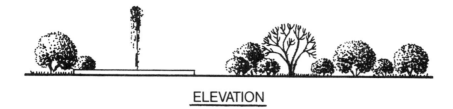

ELEVATION

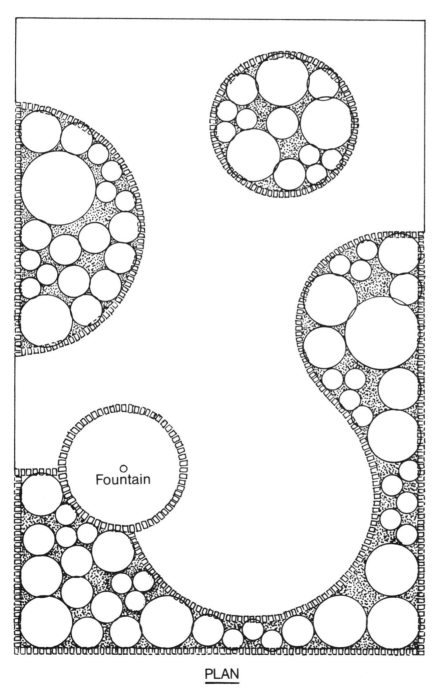

Fountain

PLAN

Fig. 8.8. Final plan for a curvilinear terrace, also showing elevation

Shown in Fig. 8.9 is a grid pattern superimposed on the pedestrian area of the terrace. The lines could represent a scored effect throughout the concrete surface in conjunction with full-depth expansion joints or perhaps 2 in × 4 in. redwood dividers, serving as expansion joints and thus creating a visually stronger pattern. The combination of straight lines and curves provides an effect compatible with both angular architectural features and the curvilinear forms of nature.

Earth mounds in or near a garden setting may range from several inches to several feet in height, thus breaking the monotony of flat terrain. The convexed configurations often are effective in creating an illusion of greater distance between given points (more total surface area). Mounds may create a sense of enclosure, thereby suggesting privacy. The third-dimensional aspect of knolls and ridges, in conjunction with various plantings, serves to define, or establish the perimeter of, flat open spaces, much like wall partitions determine rooms in buildings (see Chapter 5).

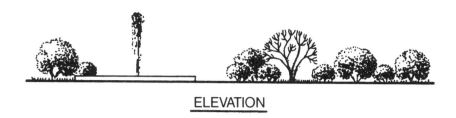

ELEVATION

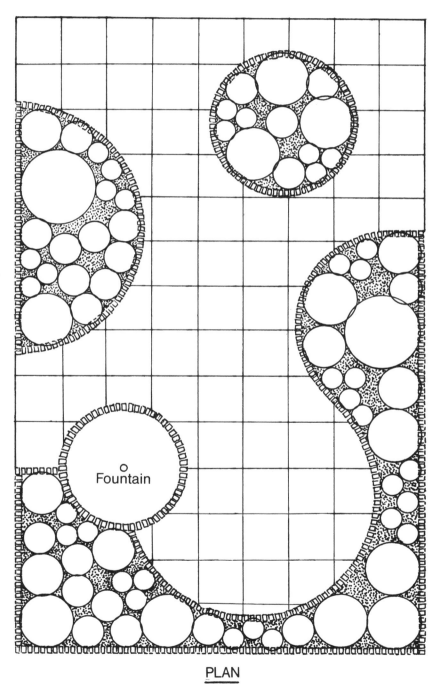

PLAN

Fig. 8.9. A curvilinear terrace with patterned surface

A Naturalistic Mound Garden

In the preliminary plan for a mound garden shown in Fig. 8.10, the mounds themselves are delineated with a continuous curving motion, both the arm and hand of the designer being held freely in the air. Re-trace the motions over and over several times so that the basic outline of each mound is fluid, never forced. Each succeeding contour should indicate a slope no greater than 3:1 for grassed areas to accommodate mowing, nor greater than about 2:1 for planted areas. Essentially, mounds are positioned on the periphery of the garden plot, thus defining the development area, affording privacy within, and at least partially screening objectionable views without.

The final plan (Fig. 8.11) for a naturalistic mound garden reveals two outdoor "rooms" (flat areas), one being more intimate or enclosed than the other. The surface of the flat areas might very well be grassed, depending on the volume of foot traffic and, of course, the desired effect. For extensive use, the development could represent a hard-surfaced patio, or possibly a "mini-mall," accommodating benches, fountains, and display panels within a cluster of retail shops.

The stippled texture of the mounds indicates ground cover and/or wood chips. The various circles represent a mixture of evergreen and deciduous shrubs, the selection of which is governed by the desirability of color, fragrance, specific screening qualities, etc., not to mention the individual species' preferences regarding soil, moisture, and exposure.

The success of garden designs in part depends on an effective circulation system. Access points first must be established. The routing of people within the garden obviously should lead them where you want them, whether the attraction be a distant vista or the prominence of garden features such as fountains, statues, flowering plants. Either pedestrians are enticed to wander in various directions through interest and intrigue, coupled with the presence of well-defined walkways, or they are discouraged from pursuing certain directions by physical barriers and/or the absence of established routes. Furthermore, the garden should not be viewed in its entirety from a single vantage point, depending, of course, on the dimensions of the development, but rather, through a progression of visual experiences, one leading to another. Earth mounds serve to direct people movement and to arouse curiosity by obscuring vision, in combination with plantings: What lies beyond? The effect of mounds perhaps is well-illustrated in the "elevation" of Fig. 8.11.

38'

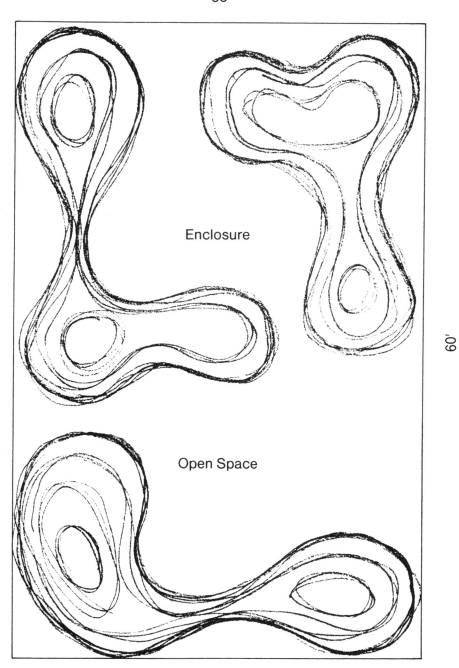

Enclosure

Open Space

60'

Fig. 8.10.   Preliminary plan for a mound garden

ELEVATION

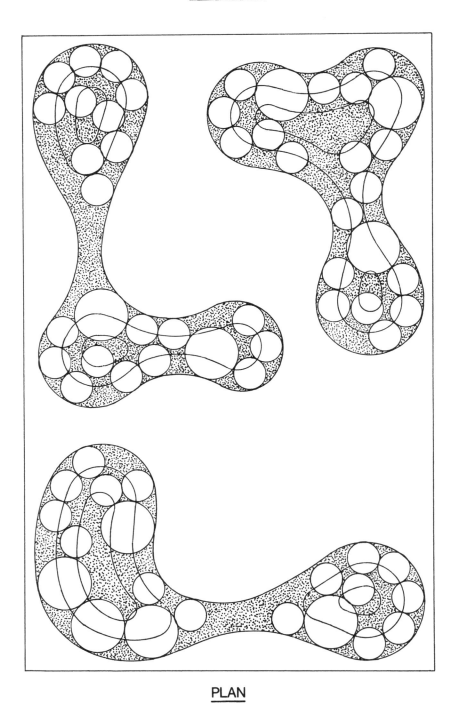

PLAN

Fig. 8.11. Final plan for a naturalistic mound garden, also showing elevation.

The number and variety of plants used in landscape compositions varies according to function and subsequent spacing. The first consideration quite simply is the need for plants. What is their purpose? Second, how shall plants be arranged most effectively to accomplish specific objectives?

One must become familiar with the growth characteristics of individual plant species and their ultimate size. Generally, gardens in later years appear overplanted, resulting from too many plantings initially, plus possible additions and/or insufficient spacing. Crowded conditions can be remedied by proper pruning and perhaps the removal or transplanting of alternate shrubs, leaving room for the remaining specimens to fully mature. The purchaser of nursery stock must consider size versus cost; larger, more expensive plants produce the intended effect almost immediately, whereas smaller specimens cost less but obviously require more time to develop. In preparing planting plans, designers often overlap the circles representing various shrubs; this in itself suggests a crowded situation usually intended only for absolute screening.

Frequently a preliminary planting consideration involves the screening of objectionable views from the proposed development site. A common approach is to establish a straight row of closely spaced evergreens; the results are positive, but the vegetative alignment often seems artifically contrived, while at the same time restricting air circulation. Essentially, a single tree placed between two points serves to screen one point from the other. One's attention is directed to the nearest object (tree), and at least momentarily the observer becomes oblivious to the background. Psychologically, the tree becomes the center of concentration, and the outlying distractions become a blur, much like a camera focusing on an object at close range. Depending on the proximity of that which is to be screened and the degree of unpleasantness, a limited number of trees and/or shrubs, informally arranged (staggered, shot-gun fashion), should suffice. (Fig. 8.12)

Within the over-all garden composition, a single, isolated plant appears conspicuously detached from the group. Two identical shrubs side by side compete with each other; neither is dominant. It may be assumed that groups of threes and fives (odd numbers) of the same species are most effective aesthetically (Fig. 8.13); larger quantities become massed, or at least the human eye cannot discern individual specimens at a glance.

Generally, each plant in a garden setting should be recognized; if its absence would not detract from the composition, then that particular plant becomes superfluous. Even when plants are massed for specific effects, the individual specimens

Tree line

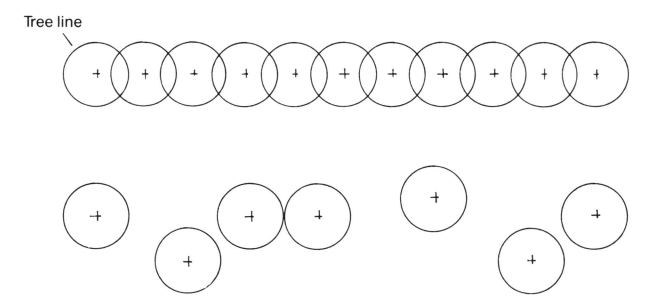

Fig. 8.12. Screening techniques. (*Top*) Absolute screening (unnatural); (*bottom*) subtle screening (natural).

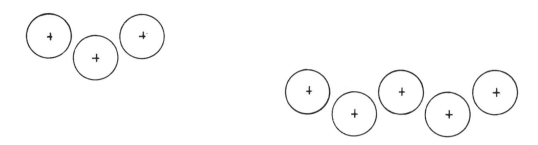

Fig. 8.13. Effective numerical combinations

should be allowed sufficient space to develop uniformly on all sides. Often plants become leggy and leafless in certain areas because of over-crowding.

Landscape styles reflect the manner in which outdoor settings are conceived. Regional climate, topography, technical knowledge, the availability of materials, social customs, affluence, and aesthetic sensitivities generally govern any particular philosophy of design or mode of artistic expression. Certain styles become fashionable, establishing a trend, which in turn may become identified with a particular period in history; traditional architecture has been associated with various cultures throughout the world. The French and Italian styles of exterior design were characterized by the imposition of humanized formality, whereas the dominant English style of the eighteenth century stressed "abhorrence to a straight line," i.e., naturalistic informality. Small-scale geometric gardens adorned with a profusion of flowers are reminiscent of a traditional style in Holland. The elements of water, color, and shade typically afford respite from the noonday Mediterranean sun. Each quadrant of our planet manifests unique methods of habitation.

The conception of original contemporary landscape architectural works should evolve from an awareness of indigenous materials, modern technology, the practical aspects of the development program, and, of course, maintenance costs. The character of existing buildings obviously should influence landscaping treatments. Too often, inappropriate period styles are borrowed from the past for the mere sake of "identity." For example, colonial structures requiring relatively flat terrain frequently are superimposed on somewhat severe slopes. The subsequent terracing of formal gardens would most likely appear artificially contrived, not to mention the problems of grading and erosion control involved. Understandably, the landscape architect often finds himself (or herself) in a kind of creative "straightjacket," having been called on after the fact, so to speak. Pretentious, eclectic art forms simply become eyesores if not modified and adapted to differing localities and the changing world.

Students of design, as well as established practitioners, must become less concerned with the application of historical precedents per se, concentrating instead on the underlying principles supporting various theories of creativity. The prototypes of another day and another place should be studied, not copied. A sense of tradition serves well only to stimulate new thinking.

Suggested Readings

Chapter One

Encyclopaedia Britannica: Vol. 10, Geochemistry; Vol. 17, Petrology; Vol. 20, Soil; William Benton, Publisher, Chicago, 1959.

Larousse Encyclopedia of the Earth, Second Edition, Paul Hamlyn Limited, London, 1965.

Lowndes, W. S., *Building Stone*, Fourth Edition (Architecture, Division 1, International Correspondence Schools), International Textbook Company, 1960.

Operations Preliminary to Building, Fourth Edition, International Textbook Company, 1958.

Chapter Two

Edmond, J. B., Senn, T. L., Andrews, F. S., *Fundamentals of Horticulture,* Fourth Edition, McGraw-Hill Book Company, New York, 1975.

Fuller, H. J., *General Botany,* Fourth Edition, Barnes & Noble, Inc., Publishers, New York, 1963.

Lehninger, A. L., *Biochemistry,* Second Edition, Worth Publishers, Inc., New York, 1977.

Northen, H. T., *Introductory Plant Science,* Second Edition, The Ronald Press Company, New York, 1958.

Encyclopaedia Britannica, Vol. 17, Photosynthesis; Vol. 18, Plants and Plant Science; Proteins; Protoplasm; William Benton, Publisher, Chicago, 1959.

Chapter Three

Taylor's Encyclopedia of Gardening, Fourth Edition, Norman Taylor (Editor), Houghton Mifflin Company, Boston, 1961.

Encyclopaedia Britannica, Vol. 1, Acids and Bases; Vol. 2, Atom; Vol. 4, Carbonic Acid and Carbonates; Vol. 9, Fertilizers; Vol. 14, Lime; Vol. 16, Nitric Acid and Nitrates; Vol. 18, Proteins; William Benton, Publisher, Chicago, 1959.

Baumgardt, J. P., Fertilizer conversion factors, *Grounds Maintenance,* Intertec Publishing Corp., Kansas City, Missouri, February, 1978.

Columbia-Viking Desk Encyclopedia, Third Edition, Viking Press, New York, 1968.

Edmond, J. B., Senn, T. L., Andrews, F. S., *Fundamentals of Horticulture,* Fourth Edition, McGraw-Hill Book Company, New York, 1975.

"Home Lawns," "Soil Fertility and Management," The Pennsylvania State University, College of Agriculture, Extension Service (Correspondence Courses), University Park, Pennsylvania.

Masterton, W. L., and Slowinski, E. J., *Chemical Principles,* Fifth Edition, W. B. Saunders Company, Philadelphia, 1981.

Chapter Four

A Handbook of Agronomy, Cooperative Extension Service Agronomists, Virginia Polytechnic Institute, Blacksburg, Virginia, 1966.

All about Lawns, Ortho Books, Chevron Chemical Company, San Francisco, 1979.

Bush-Brown, J., and Bush-Brown, L., "Soils and Soil Improvement," *America's Garden Book,* Charles Scribner's Sons, New York, 1958.

Lawns and Ground Covers, A Sunset Book, Lane Book Company, Menlo Park, California, 1964.

ProTurf, Scotts Research Center, Marysville, Ohio.

Turfgrass Guide, Virginia Polytechnic Institute and State University, Blacksburg, Virginia, 1975.

Chapter Six

An Inexpensive Economical Solar Heating System for Homes, U.S. Department of Commerce, Springfield, Virginia, 1976.

Grounds Maintenance, Intertec Publishing Corp., Kansas City, Missouri, March, 1981.

Chapter Seven

Graves, M. E., *The Art of Color and Design,* Second Edition, McGraw-Hill Book Company, New York, 1951.

Hubbard, H. V., and Kimball, T., *An Introduction to the Study of Landscape Design,* Hubbard Educational Trust, Boston, 1959.

Ortloff, H. S., and Raymore, H. B., *The Book of Landscape Design,* M. Barrows & Company, Inc., New York, 1962.

Chapter Eight

Encyclopaedia Britannica, Vol. 13, Landscape Architecture; Vol. 15, Mondriaan, Pieter Cornelius; William Benton, Publisher, Chicago, 1959.

Index